MY DAYS WITH BAASHA

MY DAYS WITH BAASHA

THE RAJNIKANTH PHENOMENON

Suresh Krissna

Malathi Rangarajan

Westland Ltd

westland ltd
Venkat Towers, 165, P.H. Road, Maduravoyal, Chennai 600 095
No. 38/10 (New No.5), Raghava Nagar, New Timber Yard Layout, Bangalore 560 026
23/181, Anand Nagar, Nehru Road, Santacruz East, Mumbai 400 055
93, 1st Floor, Sham Lal Road, Daryaganj, New Delhi 110 002

First published in India by westland ltd 2012

10 9 8 7 6 5 4 3 2 1

ISBN: 978-93-81626-29-0

Photographs courtesy:
Kavithalayaa Productions Pvt. Ltd; Film *Annamalai*—Shri K. Balachander and
Mrs Pushpa Kandaswamy
P.A. Art Productions; Film *Veera*—Shri Panchu Arunachalam and Mr Subbu
Sathya Movies; Film *Baasha*—Shri R.M. Veerapan and Mrs Selvi Thyagarajan

Typeset in 11/15 pts. Requiem Regular by SÜRYA, New Delhi
Printed at Manipal Technologies Ltd, Manipal

This book is dedicated to filmgoers all over the world.
Without you, we would be nowhere.

CONTENTS

PREFACE

Early one morning, I alighted from the train at Coimbatore Junction and walked towards an auto-rickshaw. The driver recognised me at once. 'Rajnikanth and you make an extraordinary combination—*Annamalai* and *Baasha* are proofs enough,' he said. A few years ago, standing behind me in the queue at the check-in counter at the Chennai airport, was a young man who introduced himself as a software engineer.

'Oh, hello,' I nodded.

He smiled and said, 'I must have watched *Annamalai* and *Baasha* at least twenty-five times!'

Wherever I go, reactions are similar. Be it the literate or the lay, old or young, affluent or ordinary, Rajnikanth has touched their lives through his films.

My recent interaction with film buffs for a television channel was yet another reiteration. The audience, almost all of them, voted for *Baasha* as Rajnikanth's best film till date. I was overwhelmed. Released fifteen years ago, it ran to packed houses then, but the youngsters who plumped for *Baasha* that evening must have been just seven or eight years old at the time! Yet it was foremost on their minds when they saw me!

From the auto-rickshaw driver at one end of the spectrum to the soft-spoken computer engineer and the group of enthusiastic students on the other, Rajni has impacted every stratum of viewers.

Over the years, wherever I've travelled, within the country and without, Tamil filmgoers have stopped me to find out, first-hand, about the making of *Baasha*, and the charisma of Rajnikanth.

The incredible reach of Rajnikanth, the Superstar, particularly with reference to the three films out of the four we've made together, still bowls me over. His magnetism is on unprecedented lines, and has helped many of his films gain cult status. *Baasha*, it appears, is still in the top rung in the fans' list of Rajni favourites. As a director, *Baasha* was a gratifying experience for me, but together, Rajnikanth and I seem to have woven a magical yarn for the audience that holds them in thrall to this day!

There hasn't been a single interview after *Baasha* where I have not fielded posers on the making of the film. '*Naan oru thadava sonna nooru thadava sonna maadhiri*' ('Saying it once is equal to my having said it a hundred times') is a powerful piece of dialogue in *Baasha*. 'How did you come up with that line?' is an oft-asked question.

Repeated references to the scene on the escalator in *Annamalai*, and the number, 'Maadathilae Kanni Maadathilae' ('In the balcony where young women gather'), shot on Meena and Rajnikanth in *Veera* (our second film together after *Annamalai* and again a roaring hit), have also been part of several of Q & A sessions with Rajnikanth fans. 'We heard that you had originally conceived the song very differently. Tell us about it,' they ask.

My memories of those days are still vivid. So is the plethora of positive responses to my films with Rajnikanth. These factors set me thinking. Perhaps I should pen my recollections of the times when I rubbed shoulders with the Superstar, the simple human being whom I have observed from close quarters, his whacky sense of humour, his dedication, his humaneness, and the frenzied behind-the-scene-moments we shared at work. I decided to go ahead and here they are, for you to read, savour and devour!

The insights, I'm sure, will leave fans of the Superstar elated.

Read on and enjoy the repast, as much as I did reliving the times!

SURESH KRISSNA

I

HALL OF ACTION

January 11, 1995. A day before the release of *Baasha*. We're at Albert Theatre, Chennai. The air is rife with excitement. There are huge portraits of Rajnikanth at the entrance, as well as rows of colourful pennants swaying in the wind. Producer A.V.M. Saravanan, actor Sivaji Ganesan's family, including his sons Ramkumar and Prabhu, a lead actor in his own right, Tamil film directors S.P. Muthuraman, R.V. Udhayakumar and P. Vasu, and other eminent personalities from the industry have turned up for the special screening of the film. So have fans of the actor. The full house seems to augur the stupendous success that is to come *Baasha*'s way.

Rajnikanth's wife Latha, and daughters Aishwarya and Soundarya, have arrived. I knew Rajnikanth would not be found anywhere near the venue that evening. Even now, after so many films and innumerable years of experience, Rajnikanth can never sit through a premiere of his film calmly. With anxiety writ large on his face, he is like a newcomer on the eve of his maiden release. Because, to him, every film is equally important. Such dedication can take an actor only one way—upward. And the Superstar continues to prove it time and again!

Rajnikanth is a very private person. Before the release of his film, he watches it with the main technicians once, and that's it. If there are a hundred invitees gathered for a show of a Rajni film, you will never find him there. It's been the same from the day I met him, and filmmakers are used to it. 'No point, Sir, no one can convince him to attend the show,' the crew would tell me whenever I suggested he should join us for the premiere.

But after the screening, he would call up each one of his close friends to find out their responses. 'What did you like about it? Did you find any obvious flaws? Tell me frankly,' he would ask. Not once have I heard him sound overconfident about a project. The tension he goes through before every film of his rolls out is unbelievable. And for all that, he is one actor whose films have a guaranteed opening!

Baasha was our third film together. Our combination had worked wonders at the box office on the two previous occasions, viz., *Annamalai* and *Veera*, and so the hype surrounding the third had scaled feverish heights.

The bigwigs in the film world maintain that *Annamalai*, my first film with Rajnikanth, made in 1992, was a turning point in both our careers. I cannot but agree. *Annamalai* ran without let-up for twenty-five weeks! Described as one of Rajnikanth's greatest hits, it established without doubt that he was the reigning Superstar.

Veera, our second, made in 1994, was very different from *Annamalai* in content and treatment, and yet it turned out to be another money-spinner. The feel-good film—with its ample dose of comedy and romance—was lapped up by filmgoers with the same enthusiasm they had shown to the action-packed *Annamalai*. The general verdict was that though *Veera* was enjoyable, the protagonist wasn't as heroic as in *Annamalai*.

Rajni and I were prepared for the comparison. After *Annamalai*, we knew filmgoers were enthusiastically looking forward to another bout of unbridled action from the duo of Rajnikanth–Suresh Krissna. Their expectation was natural, and initially it did worry me. Rajnikanth thought otherwise and I soon found his contention convincing. In fact, even while we were busy with *Annamalai*, the idea for *Baasha* had germinated. But Rajni told me, 'Let's play our cards carefully. When a director and hero come together for a second time, it is bound to be compared with the first. Let's shelve *Baasha* for now. *Annamalai* is emerging as a power-packed treat for my fans. If we follow it up with a similar film, the impact may not be as great as we intend it to be. Instead, let's go in for a slightly different genre, tone down the heroism in it and then return with an action-packed thriller. It will work better that way.' He was absolutely right. Just as he predicted, *Baasha* turned out to be a smash hit.

Despite *Veera* being a softer film, his fans had a hunch that Rajnikanth would go back to the dynamism of *Annamalai* in our third endeavour.

The air was fraught with frenzy and eagerness, and when the screen exploded with the logo, 'SUPERSTAR'—incidentally, the prefix was used for the first time in the credits of *Annamalai*; more on that later—the fans present went delirious with joy. They flung heaps of used lottery tickets in the air to show their excitement and their deafening whistles ripped through the hall.

The crowd was going crazy, but I stood calm. I'm not the excitable kind. Nothing ruffles me easily. Or so I thought at that moment.

Right from the day I began working on *Baasha,* I had unswerving faith in the film. I was sure it would work in a big way. But then, as it began to unfold on screen, calmness gave way to anxiety . . .

Rajnikanth's entry with the song 'Naan Autokaaran' ('I am an auto-rickshaw driver') was met with thunderous applause. I didn't know it then, but the din of whistles that refused to subside when the song was going on, exemplified the response the rest of the film was going to evoke.

The hero, Manickam, Rajni's name in *Baasha*, walks into the office of the deputy inspector general of police. The police officer's body language, which seems deferential, increases the suspense—when he sees Manickam coming in, he rises up from his seat! A flash cut to Manickam's past, in grey, shadowy, negative effect, which I had brought in more as a teaser, adds to the mystery. The DIG regains composure and slowly sits down, a cryptic exchange follows and Manickam leaves. At once the official turns round to his subordinates and asks them to bring Baasha's file to his table. 'Why does he need to open a dead man's file now,' they wonder.

I knew the scene would make a dramatic impact, and I was right. The entire audience put their hands together for Manickam, who as the flash cuts revealed, has a hitherto untold past.

I vividly remember being at my wits' end at one particular point—a scene before the intermission. If that segment was accepted, I knew the rest would be a breeze.

In the previous scene, when Manickam was dragged, tied to a lamp post and beaten up, there was stunned silence in the hall, as if to say that this can't be allowed to happen to their hero. My tension mounted. But when they noticed Manickam's disdainful smirk, the audience went into raptures. They knew their hero wasn't going to take the treatment lying down.

And a little later, when Manickam sent the villain flying into the air to hit against the very lamp post he had earlier been tied to, the entire audience, including the invitees seated in the balcony, stood up spontaneously for an ovation!

The reaction at the regular show on the following day

was even better. The crowd actually began to cheer when their Superstar was thrashed, much before he began to return the compliment!

At that moment, I knew *Baasha* had arrived!

During intermission, well-known filmmaker A. Jagannathan called me over and said, 'You've given a break at the most appropriate point. In fact, this is the best interval sequence I've ever watched. And if the tempo is maintained in the rest of the film, you can rest assured that you have a winner in your hands.'

How prophetic his words were! And what an unforgettable sojourn it has been!

From *Annamalai* to *Veera* and then to *Baasha* and beyond—those memorable days at the shooting spot with Rajnikanth have left a lasting impression. The magical moments with the charismatic star remain etched in my mind. I didn't jot down any of the experiences, then. Yet, the memories are vivid.

Fifteen years have gone by and I've wielded the megaphone for fifty-one films, but even today I'm best known as the director of *Baasha*. The spell it has cast is still very strong.

2

THE JOURNEY BEGINS

'Everything is pre-determined and divinely determined,' said a spiritual master. I wouldn't have given much thought to his words had I not experienced their veracity first-hand.

March 11, 1992 is a day that was a turning point in my career.

In the first week of March that year, a huge advertisement in the vernacular daily *Dhina Thanthi* announced: 'K. Balachander's production house Kavithalayaa proudly presents *Annamalai,* starring Rajnikanth.' The film was to be directed by Vasanth.

K. Balachander, or KB as he is known, is a veteran director in the Tamil film industry, with more than a hundred films to his credit. He has introduced innumerable actors, including Rajnikanth, and several technicians too. I'm proud to say that I am also a product of the KB school. I trained under K. Balachander for fourteen films. From the position of fifth assistant, I climbed up every rung slowly and steadily till I rose to the level of associate director, before I took off on my own.

Beginning with *Ek Duuje Ke Liye* (1981), the Hindi remake of KB's Telugu hit *Marocharitra,* that made Kamal Haasan popular in the Hindi belt, to *Sindhu Bhairavi* (1985), another landmark film in Tamil with Suhasini and Sivakumar, and *Punnagai Mannan* (1986), Balachander's films were my training ground.

At the time, unaware of the developments in my guru's camp in Chennai, I was busy wrapping up *Jaagruti,* my Hindi film project with Salman Khan and Karisma Kapoor, in Mumbai. I completed work on March 8, and left for Chennai on the morning of March 9. I was going home prepared for a long break because I hadn't signed my next film.

So I was rather surprised to see Pazhani, the manager with Kavithalayaa, waiting to receive me at the airport.

'KB wants to meet you at once,' he said.

So, from the airport I headed straight to my mentor's home. KB was in his office on the first floor. As always, the air-conditioner was on, in full blast, and the room, bitingly cold.

'Sit down, Suresh,' he pointed to the chair before him. 'I'm not going to beat around the bush. Vasanth has walked out of the project which we'd announced. We have to begin shooting the day after tomorrow. The film has to be released in June as scheduled. Kavithalayaa's honour is at stake. Will you direct Rajnikanth?'

I gaped at him. Before I could gather my wits, he

continued, 'At the last minute Vasanth has backed out saying that he will not be able to direct Rajni. Maybe he has a strong reason for saying so. What do you say?'

The poser was a bolt from the blue. I nearly went blank and the words that followed did nothing to ease my shock. 'I'm sure you will not turn down my request. I've already told Rajni that you are in. Take this amount as advance and start work straightway.'

I gazed at the brand new currency that he'd placed in a beautifully embroidered pouch. The amount was Rs 109. (I still have the money and the pouch safe with me as part of my memorabilia.) 'Natrajan and Ananthu are in the office. They'll give you the details.'

I thought of my spiritual guru, meditated for a moment, looked up at KB and said, 'Count me in, Sir. I'll do it.' He was very pleased with my reply.

My mentor, whom I hold in high esteem, is in a crisis and seeks my help. How could I refuse?

'Rajnikanth is waiting to meet you. Go ahead!' KB said. And that, to put it simply, was that.

The film was *Annamalai,* and it proved to be a pivotal point in Rajni's career and mine.

The enormity of the task before me began to sink in. The film was to go on the floors in a couple of days, and here I was, clueless about the script, dialogue, costume, cast, crew or location of the film! I had to begin from scratch!

Natrajan and Ananthu (the then pillars of Kavithalayaa) congratulated me and suggested I proceed to Hotel Woodlands to meet writer Shanmugasundaram. 'He will narrate the script,' they said.

Shanmugasundaram gave me just the gist. The story sounded interesting, but much detailing had to be done. 'We can do it in the course of the shoot, Sir,' he said. I gathered that the original plan was to develop the narration as the film progressed. My tension ought to have mounted. Instead I was smiling to myself. This race against time was actually turning out to be exciting!

As we worked together, I began to understand the extent of Shanmugasundaram's acumen in screenplay and dialogue writing. He was working in Hindi cinema with filmmaker K.C. Bokadia when Rajnikanth spotted his talent and brought him in as the writer of *Annamalai*.

A meeting with Rajnikanth had been fixed for the evening, at his residence in Poes Garden. Natrajan accompanied me. Rajni, who was sitting outside in the lawn, welcomed me with a warm smile, offered me a seat and came straight to the point.

'What do you think of the script,' he asked.

I was frank. I enumerated the positives and negatives. 'A lot of work needs to be done. *Annamalai*'s story revolves round the protagonist's ancestral home and the land attached to it. Unless the house is vested with sentimental value, Annamalai's anguish, his mother's agony and the significance of his challenge, when he sees his home being razed to the ground, will not be established effectively. The romance and comedy elements have to be spruced up. Also, the process of a milkman turning into a rich businessman has to be logical and has to happen within a suitable timeframe. But the second half seems good,' I said, and I could see that he appreciated my candour.

'Shooting is just a day away. Have they told you about it?'

'Yes, Sir. I'll have a scene ready by then and get the set, cast and other matters organised tomorrow,' I said.

Starting March 11, it was going to be ten days of non-stop shooting, followed by a four-day break. My interaction with Rajnikanth was on the evening of March 9, and at that point, only the main actors of the film—Khushboo, Manorama and Sarathbabu—had been finalised! The rest of the casting remained to be done!

During the seven years I worked under K. Balachander (1979 to 1986), he made just one film with Rajnikanth, *Thillu Mullu,* in 1981, and even during the making of it, I was with KB's unit in Mumbai. So I had hardly interacted with Rajni. In fact, I had met him only twice earlier; the first time was at Sowcar Janaki's house, where the shooting of *Thillu Mullu* was going on. Amirjan, who was working as an associate, introduced me to Rajni as KB's assistant from Bombay, working on *Ek Duuje Ke Liye*.

'How is the film shaping up,' Rajnikanth asked.

'Very well, Sir,' I replied.

His next statement came as a surprise. 'I hope the film turns out to be a super hit. The Hindi audience should know what a storehouse of talent Kamal is.'

Two great actors, contemporaries, or rather competitors, and here is one, praying for the success of the other, and praising him to the skies! My admiration for Rajnikanth began then. I thanked him and left.

The second meeting was five years later, at Rajnikanth's residence in Poes Garden. A scene for the Sivakumar–Sarita starrer *Agni Saatshi*, where Rajnikanth played himself, was being filmed. By then Rajnikanth had begun acting in Hindi films. *Andha Kanoon* had been released, and he was working in a few more. I remember asking him casually, 'How do you manage the Hindi dialogue, Sir?'

'Just as I manage Tamil,' he replied, and laughed aloud in his typical style. (Rajni hails from Karnataka and his mother tongue is Marathi.) The honesty behind the humour increased my respect for the man.

And when I met him for the third time, it was as the director of his film! At that moment, our earlier exchanges came to my mind. *He is a formidable name in cinema, and here I am, a person who has admired him from afar, all set to wield the megaphone for his film*, I told myself. Reality refused to sink in.

The discussion was over, and just as we got up to leave, I asked, 'Can I have two minutes with you in private?'

'Sure,' he said, and took me to his make-up room on the ground floor of his residence.

We sat down. He gazed at me intently, waiting for me to open up. I looked him in the eyes and said, 'Honestly, Sir, I am happy to have got this opportunity. I will be ever grateful for it. I just wish to add that I'm a friendly, egoless person. I believe a director and actor should be friends first. Our rapport alone can help the project sail smoothly. Any suggestions from you will always be welcome. Let's share our ideas and do it together. Everything will turn out well.'

He smiled, instantly got up, and shook my hand.

We left the house and I began walking a little ahead towards my car. Natrajan was behind me, and as I casually turned around, I noticed Rajnikanth showing a thumbs-up sign to Natrajan! I knew he was happy to have me on board.

3

WINNER ALL THE WAY

Annamalai had to be released in June—the release date had been announced and delaying it was unthinkable. But the time on our hands was ridiculously inadequate. It was bound to be a maddening schedule for a couple of months: shooting, dubbing, editing, re-recording and the recording of the songs had to go on simultaneously! But as I said earlier, the pressure gave me a high.

That night, when I told Chandra about the eventful day and the test that awaited me, she was flabbergasted. 'But how can you deliver?'

'If my mentor has made such a request, it only shows his confidence in me. I can't let him down,' I told her. Incidentally, Vasanth was also trained at the KB school.

The one day that I had before work began in earnest was spent organising the gala muhurat the following morning.

A set of a court hall was available and I decided to shoot the first scene there.

In an industry steeped in superstition, it is blasphemy to even think of not using the muhurat shot—the first shot canned *has* to be inserted at some point. So I suggested we begin work with Rajni breaking a coconut and praying at a temple. 'We can always use it at some stage in the film,' I told the unit. It was shot at the Lord Ganapathi temple inside AVM Studios.

Later, *Veera* and *Baasha* too took off from the same temple and soon it came to be known as 'Rajni Pillaiyar'! As several films begun at this temple have gone on to become hits, the deity is now considered an augury of success. But when I started my first Rajni film at the place, little did I expect it to gain such a status!

While on the subject of sentiment and superstition, I'm reminded of the contention regarding the title, *Annamalai*. A few in the industry had expressed misgivings about it, because of the Tamil saying, 'Annamalaikku Arohara'. Though 'Arohara' is a salutation to God, in colloquial parlance, it has gained a negative connotation as well. But KB and Rajnikanth had already decided on the title and refused to even consider changing it. Of course, once the film became a runaway hit, the name came to denote only success!

A set that was to be a teashop was put up just outside the temple, where we planned to shoot a scene with actor and comedian Janakaraj, who played Rajni's confidant in the film. Once the puja and press meet were over, Shanmugasundaram and I moved over to the inside of the 'teashop' to discuss the scene.

Suddenly I sensed Rajnikanth sitting down beside me and I stood up. But he insisted I take a seat.

'No problem, Sir,' I said.

'In that case, let me stand too,' he replied.

As the days passed, I learnt that he's a star with no airs, an actor who shows due deference to the director.

Through the first ten-day schedule, I knew my work was being observed intently by everyone concerned, particularly Rajni. Scepticism was inevitable because we had come together for the first time, and those involved had to be sure I could handle a typical Rajnikanth film, with the right ingredients of mass appeal mixed in perfect proportions.

Under normal circumstances, the way *Annamalai* shaped up is not the route a director ever follows. Most of the ideas came impromptu. Brainstorming sessions with the hero, director and assistants seated together and chipping in led to thoughts gaining form and cohesion. They were further improvised, rehearsed a couple of times and shot then and there. Such attempts could be part of practical examinations at institutions such as the National School of Drama, where, I've heard, students are given situations which they are expected to develop and enact in a matter of minutes. But here was a mammoth project that was turning out to be an extemporaneous exercise!

What gave us the guts to venture into it in such a fashion with hardly any homework done or preparation in place? Was it the confidence that Rajnikanth's charisma would see us through? Or was it my faith in the Almighty? I can't say. I only know that an unseen force spurred us on. The making of *Annamalai* beat all kinds of rationale in filmmaking!

That the hero and I barely knew each other, and had just met two days earlier, wasn't a deterrent at all. Things were progressing so perfectly that I found it hard to believe. The rapport that Rajnikanth and I struck contributed a lot to the film getting completed on time. That it went on to become a success is history. And our friendship that was forged then continues to this day.

After the muhurat shot, the opening scene with Sarathbabu and Rajni was filmed in the 'court room'. It turned out to be thoroughly hilarious.

The scene went thus: Sarathbabu is produced in court for a minor offence. Rajnikanth enters and in his eagerness to save his friend, plays both the cross-examiner and the accused, poses questions and answers them in such an irrefutable yet light-hearted manner, that the entire court is bemused. Suddenly becoming conscious of his presumptuousness, Rajnikanth scuttles out of the court room.

Rajni did a perfect job of it, but sadly, the scene was to become a prey to the pair of scissors on the editing table. Once the film was completed, the length extended to 14,950 feet. Generally, it is restricted to 14,500 feet, which translates into approximately two hours and forty minutes of running time. The extra 450 feet meant another five minutes of viewing, which was bound to affect the pace of the film. The court sequence was entertaining, but had no bearing on the plot, and hence could be done away with. Every other scene was a vital part of the story and couldn't be touched.

The rest of the unit was very much against editing it out. 'It's too good, let's retain it,' they chorused. Rajnikanth and I felt so too, but for the betterment of the film, a decision had to be taken. So we closeted ourselves and discussed the issue. Should we sacrifice a thoroughly enjoyable, rib-tickling segment, or should we go ahead and risk the lull that it would create?

I was also apprehensive because Balachander had liked the scene very much. 'That's all right, Suresh. I'll explain it to him. Just tell me what you think about it,' said Rajnikanth.

'Frankly, nothing is more important than the final product. The scene will draw out the narration, so I think it should be removed,' I replied.

As we expected, KB remarked, 'What is this, Suresh? It is a fabulous scene. Why did you chop it?' Nevertheless it had to go. But even now, when I think of the sequence that had Rajnikanth rushing in, performing his mono-act in court and scurrying out, I can't help smiling.

4

FUN AND FRENZY

Certain scenes in *Annamalai* have left indelible impressions in the minds of viewers and the production team, albeit for different reasons—Rajnikanth's rib-tickler with the ophidian, for one. The Superstar has a way with snakes, and his comic scenes with reptiles always work. 'This man loves the creature and it looks as if the snake understands his affection and reciprocates,' I would tell myself. But that was till we began shooting the popular scene with Rajni and the cobra.

The last day of shoot before the scheduled four-day break, was to be held at Chakra House in Alwarpet, Chennai. The art director had transformed it into a women's hostel, where the scene involving Rajnikanth and a snake was to be shot. Khushboo (Subbulakshmi in the film), is a college student and an inmate of the hostel.

We had discussed the sequence in detail before we went to the spot, yet I was nervous because we were going to shoot under uncontrolled circumstances—none of us had a clue about the direction in which the snake would decide to move! And I hadn't worked in such an anxiety-filled situation before. Naturally, I was tense.

I walked up to the snake-charmer and asked him to show me the cobra he had brought with him for the shoot. And abracadabra! He took it out like a magician pulling out a rabbit by its ears from his hat. Instinctively, I recoiled in fear. God, was it long! And menacing! It was then that I observed the man from close quarters for the first time, and the butterflies in my stomach increased. The man looked anything but sober. Hiding the jitters, I asked, 'How safe is the snake to work with?'

'Very safe, Sir, I have stitched up its mouth, not to worry,' was his cool reply.

The man's tipsiness increased my anxiety. I asked the unit manager Nagappan and my associate Natraj (a close friend of Rajnikanth, he had directed the Superstar in *Anbulla Rajnikanth* and had joined our team to work with me as an associate) to double-check with him. But they were least perturbed.

'Sir, we know the fellow. He has supplied snakes for Rajnikanth's earlier films too. There's nothing to worry about,' they reassured me.

If only I could be as calm as they! Here I was, shooting Rajni with a snake after two films with Kamal Haasan. The two actors were friends, but their fans saw them as rivals. In the event of anything untoward happening on the sets, wouldn't Rajnikanth's fans bash me up? I dreaded the consequences . . .

I covered up my nervousness with a smile and prepared myself mentally for the task ahead. Somehow, intuitively, I didn't feel too comfortable about allowing the snake near Rajnikanth.

Things were set for the shoot and though I assumed an air of confidence, I was still thinking of a way to halt work. But I couldn't change the scene. It had to be done . . .

According to the story, a snake is spotted entering the hostel, and even as the girls there scream in fear, it slithers away into one of the rooms. Neither the warden nor the inmates are able to spot it. Just then Annamalai arrives at the hostel to deliver cans of milk, and the women turn to him for help.

Annamalai is petrified, but seeing no way of escape from the dangerous task, he gingerly walks in looking for the creature.

Rajnikanth entered the room, ready for the shot, and I could feel my tension mounting. I told my cinematographer, P.S. Prakash, to place the camera at the end of the room and instructed the snake-charmer to leave the creature at the centre. 'Sit near it. The moment Rajnikanth enters, you scoot,' I instructed him over and over again.

But I knew everything hinged on the route the cobra would decide to take once it was let out. The technicians were standing huddled in a corner with no way to get out in case of an emergency, unless its owner came to their rescue. Again, one look at the man and my heart sank. He appeared every inch inebriated! And completely undependable! How could I expect him to act responsibly in case of an emergency?

Pushing aside the fear and the imminent danger on hand, I uttered a silent prayer and went ahead.

I had told Prakash to use a zoom lens so that he could adjust the camera according to the demands of the situation. Rajni walked into the frame with his face creased in fear, headed straight to the place where the snake was and sat next to it with his legs crossed and eyes focused on the creature. I was chewing my nails, and I could see that the others were equally anxious.

For a few seconds the snake was still. Then, slowly, it uncoiled itself and started climbing on Rajni. From his right leg it went up to his shoulder and then to the other side of his body! All the while Rajni reacted with nervous laughter and sheepish chuckles. His expressions were so hilarious and spontaneous that I turned towards Prakash to tell him to zoom in on the Superstar's face, when I saw him doing just that! And looking through the lens he was chortling at Rajnikanth's reactions. The tension in the room eased a little. I joined Prakash in the laughter— silently, of course! We couldn't afford to upset our creeping visitor, you see!

All the while, the snake kept moving from one side to the other till it finally found its position around

Rajnikanth's neck. The Superstar's pose with the serpent around his neck reminded me of Lord Shiva. I was so engrossed in the beauty of the scene that I forgot to call out for the shot to end! Only when amidst his comic expressions Rajni shouted, 'For God's sake, cut it, man!' did I realise that I'd got carried away.

As soon as the shot was canned, I called out to the snake-charmer. 'Please take away your cobra,' I told him, and heaved a sigh of relief. He picked it up with nonchalance and walked out triumphantly amidst cheers.

The members of the unit had enjoyed the shot immensely and couldn't stop talking about it. They rushed towards Rajnikanth to congratulate him. When I got a chance I shook his hand and said, 'Your reactions were extraordinary! Very natural! Did you rehearse in private? I mean, did you plan to emote with such terrific nuances, Sir?'

Rajni queried back, 'What do you mean "planned", Suresh? Everything was real. I was terrified and the nervous laughter was a result of it!' His half-serious, half-jocular expression had me in splits.

I thought of all the tension I had gone through and realised that my initial fear had been unfounded. I smiled to myself.

But was I laughing it off too soon?

5

THE TENSION RETURNS

I explained the next shot to Prakash and went out of the set for a cup of tea. In a corner, at the other end of the house, I saw Natraj and Nagappan arguing agitatedly with the snake-charmer. Sipping the tea, I quietly walked towards them. Instead of thanking the man for his snake, which had co-operated wonderfully, why were the two shouting at him?

'What's happening?'

'Nothing, Sir, nothing at all,' Nagappan sounded perturbed. Natraj slipped off from the place.

'Arrey yaar, what do you mean nothing? Come on, I insist you tell me why this fellow is being shouted at!'

'Just a trivial payment issue, Sir, that's all.'

'Is that all? Then settle the matter amicably. I'm very happy with the way his snake performed today. And before I forget, tell him we need it for one more shot,' I said.

'Oh! No! One more shot? But Natraj said it's all over and the snake-charmer can be sent back!'

'Then he's wrong. We have a combination sequence with Rajnikanth, Khushboo and the snake,' I said. Nagappan's reaction puzzled me. 'I don't understand. Why are you getting so worked up?'

'Nothing at all, but I have to tell you, in that case we'll have to use another snake,' Nagappan said in a low voice.

I was flummoxed.

'Why? No, no! It could affect the continuity. Let's have the same creature.'

With a look of desperation, Nagappan came closer and whispered in my ear, 'Sir, please don't spread the word. There's been a mistake. This fellow hadn't sewn up the cobra's mouth as he told us. Actually the reptile that was to be used was inside the basket all the while. Instead he had taken out another snake for which he hadn't taken any precaution!'

'What are you saying? Not sewn up? So we used a snake which could have sunk its fangs into Rajnikanth and created a tragedy in front of our eyes?'

So all the while we had been enjoying the shot and watching Rajni's expressions as the dangerous creature moved all around him! I stood transfixed! So my gut feeling about the snake-charmer had been right!

The danger may sound hypothetical today, but I couldn't get over it then. My mind went berserk. What if something had happened to Rajnikanth? What a narrow escape we'd had! The moment of crisis had passed, but I reeled under the impact!

I covered up my worry and tried my best to look

composed. Now it was my turn to warn Nagappan not to breathe a word about the incident to anyone. Trying hard to smile away the shock, I went in for the next shot.

Khushboo, who goes into the room for a bath, sights the snake and opens the door screaming. Rajni rushes in just in time to see the creature crawl out of the window. He sighs in relief, looks around and becomes speechless again! Khushboo, still shivering in fear, is oblivious to the fact that she's standing with no clothes on! Only on seeing Rajnikanth's expression does she realise her state of undress . . .

Prakash kept suggesting that we should go in for a combination shot with the actors and the cobra, but I'd had enough drama for the day! Under no circumstance was I going to allow the creature anywhere near the cast!

Of course, this time it was the other snake—the one whose mouth had been safely shut—but I was in no mood for even an iota of risk anymore. I just wanted the shot over and done with. So I told him softly but firmly, 'No Prakash, I suggest the snake be canned as a separate cut.' Giving me a quizzical look, Prakash nodded.

Before the shot, Rajnikanth wanted me to brief him about the reactions I wanted from him when he notices Khushboo in the bathroom. Shanmugasundaram was ready with a piece of dialogue for the shot, but we weren't quite happy with it. I felt words were redundant in such a situation. I told Rajnikanth, 'Let's do it the way you enacted the previous sequence with the snake, without any discussion or rehearsal. Spontaneity made it work. We'll try it out the same way this time too, see what comes out of it and then decide. Let's go for the take.'

Rajni agreed.

Just before the camera began to roll, Rajni came over to me and said, 'Maybe I could keep repeating "*Kadavule, Kadavule*" ("Oh my God! Oh my God!").' The words sounded just right to me. It would convey the various emotions involved, I thought. But I also wanted to be sure that it would tickle the funny bone as much as I wanted it to. What better way to check this out than keep the people around us in the dark about the scene and observe their reactions as Rajni performed?

So we went for the take straightway.

As directed, Khushboo opened the door and yelled out, 'Help!' Next Rajni entered and reacted to the moving snake. Khushboo showed the right amount of fear at first, and then relief on seeing it slither out of the window. As instructed, she followed it up with an expression of extreme embarrassment at her bareness in front of a stranger.

Rajnikanth's stupefied look as he kept muttering '*Kadavule, Kadavule*' had the entire set, including Khushboo, doubling up in laughter.

It worked even better when Rajnikanth continued the refrain in the following shot that had him going out of the hostel, dazed.

I was sure the scene would score, and it did!

Thus, after some high-strung moments, we successfully wrapped up the schedule.

S atisfied with the outcome of the day's efforts, Rajnikanth, Prakash and I sat down to relax on the lawn, when out of the blue Rajni came out with a comment that boosted my morale no end.

'You know Suresh, I was quite apprehensive about whether you would be able to handle my kind of film, which targets the masses, but in this past week I've realised you are a director who can cater to the taste of my audience. You are the Manmohan Desai of the south. Ha! Ha!' he chortled in characteristic style. The others around joined him in the laughter, but it was I who enjoyed the words the most. His observation was a veritable stress-buster, particularly after the tension I had undergone that day. The words meant a lot to me. They still do.

I realised that my litmus test was over, and I had fared creditably!

6

MELODIES AND MEMORIES

The break which followed the first ten-day schedule wasn't a holiday for me—it was just that shooting had been halted for four days. But I had several other things to look into—the music of the film, for instance. In fact, even on the days we were shooting, after announcing pack up I would rush to composer Deva's place to discuss the music and oversee matters regarding recording of the songs.

This was the first time Deva was composing music for a Rajni film. KB's production house Kavithalayaa had had serious differences with Ilaiyaraja during the making of *Pudhu Pudhu Arththangal*, the film they brought out before *Annamalai*. Till then, Ilaiyaraja had been the music composer of all Rajni films produced by Kavithalayaa. But KB decided not to go with him for the new projects. The production house was making three films simultaneously: *Annamalai*, which came to me, *Roja*, which was being directed by Mani Ratnam, and *Vaanamae Ellai*, with KB himself as director.

KB roped in Deva as the composer for *Annamalai*, M.M. Keeravani (also known as M.M. Kreem to Hindi cinemagoers, and as Maragathamani in Tamil cinema) from Telugu cinema for *Vaanamae Ellai*, and on Mani Ratnam's recommendation, introduced A.R. Rahman for *Roja*. Deva had already been signed on for the music of *Annamalai*, by the time I came into the picture. Though Deva was making music for cinema then, a Rajni film was a giant leap in his career. In fact, many in the industry were shocked at KB's choice of Deva.

Rajni was also a little worried. Deva was new to me too, because for my first film, *Sathya*, and my Telugu projects, *Prema* and *Indrudu Chandrudu*, it was Ilaiyaraja who had been the composer.

When I met Deva to discuss the music of *Annamalai*, he had already had a session with Vasanth, who was to have directed the film. The music for the duet, 'Annamalai, Annamalai, Aasa Vechaen Unnaamala' ('I've been pining for you, Annamalai'), alone had been composed.

Deva's amiable and ever-smiling demeanour and his positive approach to work impressed me. We hit it off at once, and our friendship has only grown stronger over the years. Deva is a wonderful human being and a composer with absolutely no airs. His capability, combined with his down-to-earth nature, make him my first choice among composers. Beginning with *Annamalai*, and barring *Sangamam* (1999) and *Baba* (2002), which had A.R. Rahman's score, I've always plumped for Deva. His *Baasha* numbers are my all-time favourites. Our partnership has continued till my film *Aarumugam* in 2009. I took him along with me to the Telugu, Kannada and Malayalam films that I directed.

Every number in *Annamalai* was conceived and canned with care. We would sit together as a group and discuss the sequences, though most of the time it was Rajni and I who were on the job. It is teamwork that yields the best results. When each person involved comes out with a relevant thought that betters the previous suggestion, the final output is bound to be commendable. That was how *Annamalai* gained a winning shape.

'Vandhaenda Paalkaaran' ('Here I come, a milkman'), the opening number that introduced Rajnikanth as Annamalai to the audience, was the first song we took up. Till then, no Rajni film had had a brisk opening song to introduce the hero. I wanted it because the movie would then begin with a bang, revving up the spirit of fans from the word go. That other films followed suit and had their heroes making a dramatic musical entry, is a given. But on that score, *Annamalai* is a pioneer of sorts.

The concept for the song came from Rajni. 'I've read a poem in Kannada which talks of the cow as a deity, useful to man in so many ways. Why don't you try it out in Tamil,' he asked Vairamuthu, who was penning the lyrics of *Annamalai*. And sagacious as he is, Vairamuthu grasped the core of the poem and embellished it further, adding an element of contrast between the ever-giving cow and selfish humans who only take from other beings. He also inserted a few ingenious words to boost Rajni's image as a mass hero of the Tamils. Can you ever forget Rajni's salutation to the people of the state in the line, *Ennai vaazha vaithadhu Tamizh paalu*? ('It is the milk of love from you Tamils that has given me life.')

The words floored filmgoers!

Generally you would expect a milkman's song to be filmed in a cowshed or on the streets as he goes about his daily chores of tending the cows and supplying milk to various households. But being an ardent Rajnikanth fan myself, I wanted to see him emerge in style in this song, even if it was in a simple costume.

Having lived in Mumbai for the most part of my youth, the influence of Hindi cinema in the song sequences of my films is always strong. I wanted 'Vandhaenda Paalkaaran' to be as lively and colourful as a cheerful Amitabh Bachchan song.

As a person with an ear for music, I take a keen interest in the song sequences in my films. My penchant for round trolley shots, à la Subhash Ghai and Manoj Kumar, surreptitiously enters my music sequences. Shots like the ones seen in *Karz, Upkaar* and *Purab Aur Paschim* are bound to work here too, I felt.

'Let's do it my way, Sir. Anyway, songs are mere fantasy,' I told Rajnikanth. And off we went to Ooty to shoot this and a couple of other song sequences.

In hindsight, the milieu of the 'Vandhaenda Paalkaaran' sequence could seem illogical, but the fact is, the audience enjoyed their Superstar in action on the verdant hills with his cows and other herdsmen around. Not even the critics so much as mentioned the incongruity of the backdrop. What mattered was Rajnikanth's magic that oozed through the frames! Of course, we lined up a few cows and had hay stacked here and there to give a semblance of authenticity to the sequence. But I'm sure even without such props it would have worked in a big way. Such is this hero's draw!

It was around this time that the inimitable dancer, choreographer and actor Prabhu Deva was coming out of his father Sundaram's shadow. Sundaram was an ace in choreography. Even today his repertoire of dance sequences continues to stand apart. It is a connoisseur's treat to watch actors shake a leg to Sundaram's steps.

Prabhu Deva was assigned to handle the footwork of the 'Vandhaenda Paalkaaran' number, and the up-and-coming dancer's innovative choreography, which transported the sequence to great heights, proved that he is a chip off the old block.

Rajnikanth was supposed to begin the dance with a wink at the camera. I was so impressed with the shot that I said, 'We'll freeze this frame later. Let Rajnikanth pause and prolong the wink for a second.'

'Why, Suresh?' asked Rajni.

'It's a song for the masses. They'll be thrilled to see you do it because it will seem as though you are looking directly at them. Why not allow your fans to enjoy it for a second or two more?'

So after the wink we allowed a moment for the audience to clap, and then proceeded with the rest of the song. It was received with a deafening ovation at the cinema halls, just as I'd expected. For viewers, it established a direct connect with their hero on screen.

And for the line *Ennai vaazha vaithadhu Tamizh paalu*, we had Rajnikanth looking straight into the camera and holding his hands in supplication, as if thanking the audience. Once again they went into raptures. The gimmicks paid off really well.

We repeated the ploy later for the 'Kondaiyil Thazhambu' number. Rajni pauses for a moment after the rhetorical line, '*Koodaiyil enna poo?*' ('What is the name of the flower in her basket?'), as if asking his audience to react, before he takes off with the reply, 'Khushboo!' Such minor interactions with the audience really caught on and became a trend.

The postures, freezes and style that Prabhu Deva brought in became so popular that, after *Annamalai,* the young dance master became a name to reckon with in the film firmament.

Shooting a routine song and dance on the lead pair is not my cup of tea. So for the duet 'Annamalai, Annamalai, Aasa Vechaen Unnaamala' ('Annamalai, I pine for you'), I suggested we split up the sequence. Rajnikanth could play a bandit first, a prince on a chariot next, and then a rich, stylish guy. The differences in appearance had a bearing on the screenplay too. Prabhu Deva liked the idea. Prakash came up with suggestions about the colour combinations that would go well with the scene, and the lighting that would add to the impact— he was keen to shoot the song at dawn, and again at dusk from around six to seven. The costume designer was also asked to join the discussion and get the wardrobe ready.

As I said, we were shooting in Ooty, and it was a race against time. Completing schedules as quickly as possible was the priority. So braving the cold, we were up very early and filmed the 'Annamalai, Annamalai' duet from 4.30 to 6.30, dispersed for breakfast, got things in place for the next part of the job, and assembled for the shooting of the solo, 'Vandhaenda Paalkaaran', from eight in the morning till four in the evening. Prakash then began setting up the lights for the duet, and by six we were all ready for the shoot which went on till a few minutes past seven.

On the last day, we shot 'Prince' Rajnikanth and 'Princess' Khushboo on a chariot at the Fern Hill Palace Hotel and then wound up work. Later we canned the matching shots at Sivaji Gardens, in Chennai. Thus we completed two song sequences simultaneously in a matter of five days! Later, when the songs became chartbusters, and the sequences were raved about, our joy knew no bounds.

Prabhu Deva felt that the 'Annamalai, Annamalai' piece ought to be shot in slow motion. When working on the Kamal Haasan film, *Punnagai Mannan*, for which I was KB's assistant, I was very impressed with the novel idea that Kamal came up with for the filming of the 'Mamavukku Kuduma Kuduma' ('Give me a kiss') song, wherein the lip sync had to be perfect while the dance movements had to be extremely fast.

Technically speaking, the camera would roll at the rate of twelve frames per second, i.e., at high speed (twenty-four frames per second is normal), while the lip movement was synced with the speed of the sound, which was much less. Shooting it wasn't easy, but the result was worth it. Here, Prabhu Deva wanted the opposite effect: the movements had to be slow (forty-eight frames per second) and the lip sync normal. So sound was faster. This would actually be tougher to pull off than the sequence in *Punnagai Mannan*, but it worked brilliantly.

'Annamalai, Annamalai' was a very popular melody. Stunningly shot, the visuals increased the impact of the song. This was the time Khushboo's career graph had soared, so the pairing of Rajnikanth and Khushboo was a casting coup. Also, the costumes used in the sequence spelt elegance and style. All these put together helped make the duet evergreen.

On one of those evenings when we were shooting both 'Vandhaenda Paalkaaran' and 'Annamalai, Annamalai', I happened to notice how beautiful the sun looked, as it began setting behind the mountains. The blend of bright hues in the skyline was stunning. 'We can't let our camera miss this, Prabhu. Just make Rajnikanth walk and we'll shoot silhouettes of him. I'll insert it somewhere in the song,' I said.

The shot was included in 'Annamalai, Annamalai'. The stylish swagger against the breath-taking backdrop drew resounding applause from the audience. If such improvisations and on-the-spot decisions garnered gratifying results for us, they only proved that the popularity of *Annamalai* was ordained.

7

THE DUET THAT WAS TO BE

The 'Vandhaenda Paalkaaran' sequence opened in an interesting fashion. Rajni was made to stand behind all the dancers with his back to the camera so that when the music began, the audience couldn't spot him at once. Yet, at the cinemas, they began to scream and whistle even at that point!

Prabhu Deva seemed to know the fans' psyche, because the impact of the pose he had come up with for Rajni was terrific. The audience was sure their hero was somewhere in the periphery and would take centre-stage any moment—they found the small element of suspense exciting. And when Rajni turned round, it took quite a while for their frenzied cries to die down. At every show, at theatres in Chennai, Madurai and Tiruchi, viewers hollered for a repeat run of the song.

Originally, the script didn't allow for a Rajnikanth–Khushboo duet in the latter part of the film. But

KB wasn't too happy about it.

'The second half is on a very serious track, Suresh. Let's bring in some levity with a song on the lead pair,' he told me.

When I conveyed this to Rajnikanth, he wasn't for it. 'They are an old couple, Suresh. They have a grown-up daughter and the film has taken a grim turn. How can you bring in a duet here?'

I was caught between the two; they refused to discuss the issue directly with each other. On the one hand, KB told me, 'I insist that we have a song at this juncture. Call for Deva and get it ready,' and on the other, Rajnikanth refused to even acknowledge that a song had been recorded and we would have to include it in the film! 'We'll retain this song in the audio, not in the film,' was his response.

It looked like Rajnikanth wasn't going to relent and KB wasn't going to give up.

As work progressed, KB kept asking me, 'When do you plan to film the song I wanted? It's come out well.'

'We'll be shooting it in the end, Sir,' I would tell him.

'Oh, I see. So you plan to keep putting it off and eventually do away with it.'

'Not at all, I'll be taking it up soon,' I would assure him.

One was my mentor and the other, my hero. I didn't want to upset either.

'Suresh, listen to me. Do you know the common man's psychology? He loves to ride a bicycle with his wife sitting on the bar in front just as much as he likes to get flowers for her on his way back home every evening. It will work with our audiences. They will not think of it as an intrusion in the narration. Tell Rajni. We'll just be playing to the gallery, Suresh,' KB argued.

I was convinced, but how was I to make our hero comply?

I finally told Rajnikanth, 'Sir, he wants it. So it is better we do it.'

'All right, but where do you plan to add it?'

I conceived a situation where the song would be an extension of Khushboo's wishful thoughts . . .

It is the wedding anniversary of Annamalai and Subbulakshmi (Khushboo), and on the occasion, his mother asks the couple to pay a visit to the temple. The family is shrouded in a pall of gloom because of the treachery of his close friend, Ashok (Sarathbabu), and Annamalai is no more the cheerful man of the past. Subbulakshmi, who yearns for the fun-loving person that her husband was when she got married to him, allows her imagination to take wing, and the thoughts lead to the melodious, 'Rekkai Katti Parakudhamma Annamalai Cycle' ('Annamalai's cycle seems to have wings that make it fly').

I described the sequence that leads to the song, but Rajnikanth was far from convinced. We could think of no other option though, so he finally gave in. 'All right, Suresh. But I'll just give you one day to shoot the song, not a minute more,' he said grumpily. He still felt it would look contrived.

So one early morning, four or five shots were canned on Boat Club Road, in Adyar. In those days the area was quite deserted, so we had no problem shooting in broad daylight. The place had a slope down which Rajnikanth and Khushboo rode on a bicycle. Our next location was the Horticulture Society on Radhakrishnan Road. We worked like crazy from nine in the morning till five in the evening and completed the entire song. A real feat!

Though it was done with much reservation on our part, the audience, as KB said, seemed to like it. Another reason the song went down well with viewers was that we shot it as a quickie, cutting out the background music of the number and keeping it short. Thus it provided relief from the seriousness of the story and yet didn't affect the pace. And in a way, Rajnikanth was right. If we'd had the song running its full length of six minutes or so, it could have made the audience restless. Pruning it proved a wise decision.

Generally directors either act out every piece of dialogue and expect the cast to follow their style completely, or they explain the scene, give actors the dialogue, get them into the mood of the character and allow them to perform, suggesting changes where required.

When directing an actor of Rajnikanth's stature, I would just explain the scene and he would take over. If I observed a mannerism or a modulation that he had already done in a film and hence looked repetitive, I would point it out. He would re-enact the scene with changes and go ahead once I gave the green signal. Never would he get defensive and insist on performing the way he felt best, because he knew that both his interest and mine lay in coming out with a good final product. It was a healthy work culture that we adopted—not a case of one-upmanship.

I've never had issues with the stars I've directed. It's been the same with crews. I maintain that it is the way you put your point across that matters. Curtness can get you nowhere.

I faced a trying situation when I tried to infuse a semblance of rationale into the 'Kondaiyil Thazhambu, Nenjiley Vazhapoo' ('With the flower of the screw-pine in your hair and the flower of the plantain tree in your hand') number. Vairamuthu, the lyricist, had written the number as a peppy piece, because 'Annamalai, Annamalai' was soft and more melodic. But I was confounded when I heard the lyric, particularly the line *Koodaiyil enna poo . . . Khushboo* ('What is the name of the flower in your basket? Khushboo'). The obvious reference to the heroine irked me. And then Khushboo's lines went, *Veerathil mannan nee, vetriyil kannan nee, endrumae raja nee . . . Rajni* ('You are always a brave and victorious king, oh, Rajni').

Annamalai and Subbulakshmi are lovers and they break into a duet—fine. But what is the logic behind the two calling out to each other as 'Khushboo' and 'Rajni'? They aren't playing themselves in the film, are they?

Yet everyone else seemed quite happy with the lyric. I often recall with a smile Panchu Arunachalam's comment about the song. 'By making a hero like Rajnikanth utter her name several times, you've created a cult status for Khushboo,' he told me.

I thought I would tone it down by making it appear as Janakaraj's imaginary sequence—he played Rajnikanth's friend in *Annamalai*. But the idea didn't find favour with the rest of the team.

I struck upon another concept. In those days, you had men on bicycles with a bioscope fixed on the carriers, and people could pay and watch pictures as in a slide show. 'Let's have it as a lead-in for this sequence with Rajnikanth and Khushboo looking at various stills of themselves from other films,' I said, and finally that's the way we shot it.

I give equal importance to all the sequences in my films. And a lot of thought goes into the scenes, whether they're serious, funny, trivial or musical. The efforts have earned plaudits for me from many a quarter.

In this context I'm reminded of Allu Arvind's observation. Arvind is Telugu cinema's mega star Chiranjeevi's brother-in-law. He is a renowned producer, who has made big films such as the Aamir Khan hit *Ghajini*, and is the father of the popular young Telugu hero, Allu Arjun.

'I've been following all your films, Suresh. They may win or lose, but as a director your work can never be faulted. The script may fail you, but you are always sincere,' he told me. The words keep ringing in my ears.

8

CHALLENGE WELL MET

When we sat down to complete work on the solo, 'Oru Pennpura', Deva played out the tune he had kept ready for us. *Thanathaanana . . . thannaana . . . thannaana thana . . .* Beginning it as a sober strain, he followed it up with a mellifluous faster pace, which I found mesmerising.

'It's lovely, but the latter part of the Pallavi takes off rapidly. I can't spoil the beauty of the tune by filling it up with flippant phrases, and I'll end up doing exactly that if the tune has such short notes. So I don't think I can write the lyric for this song,' Vairamuthu said.

I was taken aback. I looked at Deva. From the quizzical expression on Deva's face, I could see that he was confused too. It was obvious that Vairamuthu was complimenting Deva's tune. There couldn't be any possible reason for his hesitation. Just a mood swing, perhaps . . .

'What happened, Vairamuthu? Don't tell me you can't do it,' I tried coaxing him.

'You've come up with excellent verses for more complicated tunes. This should be child's play for you,' Deva joined me. But Vairamuthu was firm.

At this point Rajnikanth intervened. 'Come on, Vairamuthu. Your ability with words is too well known for us to believe your argument now. You've proved your skill time and again. Just set aside your mental block and you'll come up with great lines,' he cajoled him. The praise was sincere and Vairamuthu realised it. Also, once Rajnikanth joined us in talking him into it, Vairamuthu had no choice but to agree. After all, none can refuse a request from the Superstar!

Sung by K.J. Yesudas the first stanza was:

Oru pennpura . . . thanneeril thallaada . . . en ullam thindaada . . . enna vaazhkaiyo . . . sumai thaangiyae sumai aanadhae . . . endhan nimmadhi ponnadhae . . . manam vaaduthae

(A young female dove struggles in the waters of infatuation and my heart finds the agony unbearable/ What kind of existence is this?/My emotional anchor has now become an onus/My peace is lost/I am distraught)

Vairamuthu may have settled down to write with reluctance, but the verses he penned were outstanding. They were so good, it became a challenge to conceptualise a sequence to precede the song. I needed a power-packed scene to do justice to the poignant melody that would follow it.

Annamalai has just learnt that his daughter (Dakshayani played the part) has fallen in love with the son of Ashok, his friend-turned-foe. He's shocked. He walks into his house calmly, and calls out for a cup of coffee. Exercising tremendous restraint he sits down beside his daughter and patiently tries to dissuade her from continuing her association with the boy. The daughter is adamant. He tries to din sense into her, but she is no mood to listen to him. Slowly his anger reaches a crescendo and he turns around to give her a stinging slap . . .

This was the way Rajnikanth and I envisaged the segment prior to the song. We had closeted ourselves in the make-up room and worked it out. I then came out of the room and straightway called out for the camera to roll. I had already briefed everyone about the scene, though no one in the set had any inkling about the slap that was to fall on Dakshayani's face. We kept it a secret only because we wanted the reactions to be spontaneous.

Even the other actors—Manorama, Khushboo and Dakshayani—were kept in the dark. Dakshayani was relatively new—she had done only a couple of films before *Annamalai*. Karan, a well-known leading man in Tamil cinema today, was paired opposite Dakshayani. Incidentally, *Annamalai* was Karan's first film; he was an aspiring hero then.

In an emotional scene, generally the protagonist faces the camera and delivers his lines so that the viewer understands the extent of his anger. I felt we should do the opposite. So, as the decibel level of his voice rose, Rajnikanth slowly moved away from the camera. This way the viewer would get to see only Rajnikanth's profile, and the eagerness to watch his reaction in full would increase with every passing moment. Tantalising the viewer for a while before allowing him to witness the full import of Rajnikanth's wrath should make a great impact, I felt. And it did.

Dakshayani didn't expect the slap. Neither did Manorama nor Khushboo. Spontaneously they rushed towards Rajnikanth and tried to pull him away before he could hit Dakshayani again.

Behind the camera, Prakash couldn't figure out the commotion because he hadn't been briefed about the slap either. Once the shot was over, the entire set was enveloped in silence for a second, after which there was thunderous applause.

Rajnikanth is one actor who can carry off any costume convincingly. The milkman's garb of a simple kurta sits as well on his shoulders as a classy blazer does. If black becomes him, so does white. His fit physique is the reason.

Suited and booted he looked stunning in the above scene, as the sedate businessman whose ire becomes uncontrollable when his self-respect is at stake.

After the altercation, Rajnikanth drives out of the house in a fit of fury. I love the shot where you can see him park his car on a mound and get out. Standing alone against the backdrop of nature, his pose is a picture of eloquence. The combination of alluring colours—red car, golden sunset, lush greenery and brown sand all around—makes the scene bewitching.

At this point in the sequence, I suggested to Deva that any music in the background would be redundant— silence seemed sound enough. So everything is still, except for the lone shepherd's song that falls on his ears and moves past him . . .

After a while, regaining his composure, Rajnikanth returns home. He notices his wife, mother and daughter, each seated in a different corner, brooding. He walks towards his daughter, and the scene dovetails into the song, 'Oru Pennpura'.

As it was an emotion-driven sequence, I felt a choreographer was superfluous. It had to be sheer drama. So I decided to direct the expressions, movements and the static positions of the main actors my way. Thankfully, the effort won me several compliments.

I wanted masked shots for the lines:

Kattaan tharaiyil oru thundai virippaen/Thookkam kannai sutrumae/Adhu andha kaalamae/Meththai viriththum/Suththa paneer theliththum/Kannil thookum illaiyae/Adhu indha kaalamae . . .

(Those were the days when I would spread a towel on the rough ground and fall asleep at once/Now I lie on a soft bed in comfort/But sleep eludes me.)

In the course of the song, Rajnikanth relives his past as a cheerful milkman, with not a worry in the world. I wanted the scenes projected as long shots and juxtaposed with his present predicament. As the lyric was vital for the mood of the song, I had to have the rich and sober Rajnikanth mouthing the words in the foreground, even as his mind takes him to his carefree past. Hence masking was imperative.

Today, we've made giant strides technically, and blue matte or green screens are effective options. But in 1992, the situation was different—the task took time.

To shoot actors in dual roles, the cinematographer covered a portion of the lens with black paper and filmed the scene with the exposed part. Once it was completed, he would rewind the film to the exact starting point, cover the other side of the camera, and re-shoot the scene with the actor playing the other part. Meticulous planning and precise execution were essential. Unless the cinematographer was completely confident, canning such shots was impossible.

Prakash was a wizard at getting things ready in a jiffy with available material. He cut out a black sheet, masked one side of the camera and went ahead with the shot.

The impact of the melody and the words was dramatic. And I was very pleased when I found the audience responding to the sequence warmly.

After three days of shooting the song, we got the print ready. I proceeded to the editing room to take a look at the sequence, oblivious to the jolt that was in store for me.

Ganesh and Kumar, the editors, were waiting with anxiety writ large on their faces.

'Any problem,' I queried.

'Plenty, the entire song is out of sync,' they replied. Also, as I had packed the song with lengthy shots, they couldn't cut and adjust them. The result was that every third line of the song lost connection with Rajni's lip movement. Possibly, the nagra operator had not used a fully-charged battery. So thanks to him, we were in a soup. Nagra is a portable, professional audio recorder used for motion pictures. The equipment, which normally runs at the speed of twenty-four frames per second in a song recording, had gone awry. Hence the lip movement of Rajnikanth was completely out of sync.

Anyway it wasn't the time for a blame game. I had to find a way out and find it fast. Re-shooting the sequence was impossible.

Next time you get a chance to catch *Annamalai* on television or DVD, watch this sequence carefully and you'll understand the wonders that can be performed on the editing table. An editor's deft fingers can play a major role in camouflaging flaws and highlighting positives.

At every point where the non-sync occurred, we needed an extra eight frames to adjust the music and the movement. We brought in slow motion, dissolves and close-ups to make the song and action appear completely in sync. At the same time, we were careful to see that the insertions were purposeful. After a few anxiety-filled hours, we heaved a sigh of relief. We had managed to make the song sequence look completely flawless.

9

VICTORY QUOTIENT

Originally, I had subscribed to the idea of having theme music that would be particularly relevant when we had to show Annamalai's career graph surging ahead from the position of a small-time restaurateur to that of a wealthy hotelier.

Annamalai declares to his erstwhile friend Ashok that he will attain an exalted position in life and be on a par with him one day. And true to his word he becomes a rich man. But I had to show him as a financially invincible business magnate without using much footage.

The time span is fifteen years, and includes several significant facets of Annamalai's life, culminating at the point where he is a grey-haired, middle-aged, well-to-do entrepreneur with a teenaged daughter. But the transition from the state of penury to the pinnacle of opulence had to be logical.

We planned a set of small sequences that showed Annamalai slogging it out with vengeance to realise his goal. He secures a bank loan and opens a small outlet to sell sweetmeats. His mother and wife help him out in the running of the shop and slowly he is able to open more branches. Business further improves and he is soon the owner of a small restaurant. But even better things are in store, and Annamalai, the ordinary milkman, becomes the director of a hotel that boasts of a five-star status.

Meanwhile, Sargunam (the role was essayed by 'Nizhalgal' Ravi), who had been working for Ashok, is forced to leave him after his deceit and misappropriation of funds at Ashok's office come to light. He now feigns loyalty to Annamalai. The gullible Annamalai takes him under his wing and his naïve sister falls in love with him. But as an entrepreneur Annamalai continues to thrive. His family now lives in a palatial home.

All these aspects of the story and more had to be covered, and so I kept shooting scenes at random. The sequences that reveal Annamalai's sky-rocketing success were shot in posh and prestigious locations such as Sea Rock Hotel, in Mumbai.

Once all the essential montages had been canned in Mumbai and Chennai, we sat down to assemble them sequentially. It was then that I discovered the footage to be too lengthy. I felt a song at this juncture would make the treatment succinct, and the segment, interesting.

Vairamuthu came up with the potent lines beginning with *Vetri nichayam idhu veda sathiyam,* to be used with several montages to show the passage of time. Deva embellished the words further with his reverberating music. And what a song it turned out to be! The translation of the opening line goes thus: 'A decisive victory awaits you/It is a promise as true as the Vedas'.

I began to feel that, to do complete justice to the song, the protagonist needed to mouth the lyric. But shooting had been wrapped up and we were in the final stage of post-production. There was no way we could shoot again. It was clear to me, though, that I couldn't allow the song to be used for the montages alone.

After much deliberation, I decided to talk to Rajni about it. I explained the fix we were in and requested him to spare a day for the shooting of the song. He heard me out and said, 'The idea is good but how can we execute it now? Don't you think it's too late in the day to have a set erected and go back for shooting?'

The production unit was equally sceptical.

'I have something very simple in mind, Sir,' I began. 'Let's have just one day of shoot. A black background, two fans for the wind-effect and a shutter, is all I require. Nothing elaborate. But the result will be worth it.' (Shutter is a device we use to create lightning.)

Prakash seconded my suggestion. 'It will be neat and effective,' he said.

Rajnikanth agreed without ado. 'It's your call, Suresh. If you feel it will work, I'm game. We'll do it tomorrow. I'll be ready in the morning.'

As promised, he walked in on time and we shot him in

various costumes, including that of a milkman. The powerful lyric was primary, so I went in for close-ups of Rajnikanth and completed the job in a day.

A director's flashes of ideas cannot be transferred to celluloid if the hero throws tantrums or resents being called back to work. But Rajnikanth is different. He was so involved in the scenes throughout the song that he came up with an admirable performance. I realised that, among other factors, his commitment and diligence have also been instrumental in making him a superstar nonpareil.

As planned, we shot the sequence with a black backdrop that had an alluring dance of light and shade. Flash cuts from Annamalai's past and inter-cuts of dialogue were added to enhance the impact. The result was wonderful.

Even now, the composition boosts the spirit of the listener. It isn't surprising that today many use the song as their mobile ringtone. The words and the music have made it an ever-rejuvenating piece.

During the course of the song, a small pencil drawing of a four-wheeler appears on screen, and grows in size into a real car. Rajnikanth, who is inside it, opens the door and gets out. We had to use special effects to make the shot possible, and as I mentioned earlier, in the year 1992, technical wizardry hadn't reached the dizzying heights it has today.

It is in this scene that, for the first time in the film, he is seen suited and booted. My satisfaction was immeasurable when I saw the audience at the cinemas shouting ecstatically, thrilled to see Annamalai win the challenge and emerge a wealthy man.

I couldn't wait to get the film processed. Once the positive was ready, I took it to the editing room. We spent the next forty-eight hours editing the shots back and forth till the sync was perfect. The excitement on the faces of my editors Ganesh and Kumar was proof that the extra effort had been worthwhile.

Finally it was over and I eagerly waited to show it to Rajnikanth. I was keen to see his reaction.

He was at the dubbing theatre in AVM Studios. The moment he came out for lunch, I said, 'I want you to see what we have for you, Sir.'

Rajnikanth is known for his spontaneous and honest observations. If he feels that a job has been done well, he showers plaudits on the doer without reservation. The surroundings matter little to him. So it was that day. I was standing behind the other technicians because I was slightly tense. But gently nudging them aside he walked towards me with a smile and gave me a hug.

'Fantastic, Suresh, simply fantastic. I've no other word to describe the work you've done,' he said. 'I never expected it to be so wonderful,' he added. He then looked at everyone around and asked, 'What do you people feel about the sequence?' And they responded with a joyous applause.

When KB saw the double positive, he particularly mentioned the way the song had been conceived. And as a technician, I was happy because the appreciation was a victory for our effort.

10

INCREDIBLE SYNCHRONY

Radha Ravi, Sarathbabu's father in *Annamalai*, has the hero's house razed to the ground when he isn't around and later humiliates him, saying he was kicking up a fuss for the destruction of a dwelling place that was nothing more than a hut—an eyesore, which didn't deserve to exist near a five-star hotel! Annamalai flares up and vows to make the family that has usurped his property in the name of friendship and rendered him homeless, pay for its atrocities.

Shanmugasundaram's dialogue for the scene was brilliant. As I was going through the script, my wife Chandra walked up to me and said, 'This scene has shaped up well and will be the talking point of the film. You can make it unforgettable by executing it differently.'

We had decided to bring in wind, rain and lightning to show that Nature was equally furious at the wrongs meted out to Annamalai. As the scene of action was the hall of Ashok's (Sarathbabu's) house, the effect of the rain battering the windows and the blinding lightning accompanying it had to be shown inside. Prakash had planned things to perfection. Yet Chandra's words set me thinking. I ought to try something more, I thought. I needed a few minutes of quiet to work it out.

Rajnikanth was lying down on a sofa in a corner of the set rehearsing his dialogue with his eyes closed and a piece of wet cloth covering his face. The practice continues to this day. The supine pose in the midst of the mêlée at the shooting spot is a norm with Rajni. He remains so till he is called to take his position in front of the camera. Any old couch, bench or ottoman on the set is enough for him. He never stirs out of the set. Neither does he seek refuge in the cosy confines of a caravan.

If Rajni has given the dates for a film, he is present on the set on all the days, patiently waiting to be called for the shot. All he needs is a Man Friday beside him, who sees to it that he isn't unnecessarily disturbed by the unit hands or by excited fans.

At the end of five minutes I walked up to Prakash. 'I want this scene to stand out for its emotional content, performances and unique filming technique. Just tell me whether my suggestion is possible,' I said, and explained my idea to him.

Generally, trolley shots with the camera on it can move straight or in a circle. If the camera has to go up and down, a crane is used. But I felt having the equipment travel in a triangle, with close-ups of the hero's fiery outbursts and wide-angle shots culminating in the slapping of his thigh as if to challenge the enemy would not only be innovative but also make a better impact.

'Rajni will stay in his position; it is the camera that should go around him in a triangle,' I told Prakash.

This experiment had to be co-ordinated with the accompanying wind, rain and lightning effects.

Prakash, one of the finest cinematographers of the time, was, as always, positive. 'It is possible, Suresh. Just give me half an hour,' is all he said, and sent his assistants to scout for empty wooden boxes in the studio. These boxes are used to transport the huge lights used in shooting. As more than fifty were needed, we borrowed them from film crews that were working on the other floors of the studio.

As I write these lines, I think of Prakash . . . it's sad he isn't alive today to relive the experiences and discuss the Rajni factor that was such a significant part of our lives!

The way we went about shooting the scene is quite technical. Yet the lay reader ought to know the diligence of the crew that made it possible. Today's scenario is very different—canning such shots is child's play. But in the early 1990s it was a tough proposition. A triangular track for a trolley shot was impossible.

As I said, trolleys for cameras move only in a straight line, i.e., from right to left or vice versa, or in a circle (we call it round trolley). The movement of the camera in a triangle had never been attempted. So a link resembling a half 'C' (a segment of the round track) was attached to the straight track. This contraption enabled the camera to move from the straight line, in a triangle, through the half 'C'. The procedure is easier said than done because the joint could cause jerks to the camera when it was in motion, which in turn could affect the clarity of the shot.

The shot in *Annamalai*, which I mention, begins with Rajni standing between two characters at a time. (Radha Ravi, Sarathbabu and 'Nizhalgal' Ravi had to take their positions in turns.) If you watch the scene you'll realise that the camera moves behind two of them, catches Rajni alone, moves closer from behind the back of the characters to zoom in on him, first to the right side of his face then to the left and then again moves back to the original position it was in, viz., behind the other two characters.

Camera tracks are laid on the ground. But Prakash placed wooden boxes on the floor and laid the track on them to keep the jerks to a minimum. Two such tracks at different levels were created. When the camera passed behind the actors and closed in on Rajni, the actors had to move out, so that the straight track could be removed and the link attached. He accomplished the task of removing and joining of the tracks with as little jiggle as possible, even as the camera was filming the shot.

The use of boxes increased the height at which the camera was placed. This meant the level of the stand holding the shutters had to be proportionately higher. Otherwise, when the shutters opened to create the lightning effect, the shadow of the camera and the workers who were pushing the trolley on the track would fall on the actors. So the four men who were assigned the task of 'creating' lightning using shutters were made to stand at a higher level.

Sarathbabu and Radha Ravi, who were to be part of the scene, came inside to hazard a guess about the commotion, and went back looking puzzled. Rajni slowly removed the piece of cloth from over his eyes to find out the reason behind the frenzied activity, and looked equally confounded.

Soon Prakash was ready. I went to Rajni and told him to stand before the camera.

'I am ready, Suresh, but I don't understand what's going on,' he said.

'The camera will move around in a triangular pattern, but don't let it bother you. You fix your eyes at the point I tell you to and begin your performance. The three actors—Radha Ravi, Sarathbabu and "Nizhalgal" Ravi— will take their positions in turns. They will clear the place and re-enter as required but you will not move. And don't pay any attention to the confusion behind you. We will be removing, re-adjusting and adding new tracks for the trolley, but you concentrate on your dialogue and expressions. Finally, the camera will close in on you,' I told Rajni.

It's easy to instruct an actor to perform an emotion-charged scene under such distracting circumstances, but for the actor, executing it is anything but! Rehearsals, with the camera movement, were not possible because the process was too complicated. Removing and replacing tracks would have been time-consuming. So we went for the take straightway. I still admire Rajni for the confidence with which he handled the scene amidst the din, and the confusion caused by other actors running in and out in front of him.

Only a single shot can bring out the intensity of such a scene, because the actor is bound to be charged with the same level of emotion throughout. Breaking it up could affect the impact. This shot was canned in a single take!

At the end of it, I was the first to put my hands together for Rajnikanth, who is not merely a stylish super hero, but also a stupendous actor. He never allowed himself to be disturbed till I called 'Cut'. Hats off to Rajni the actor, I told myself.

In those days, we didn't have monitors to give the director a clear view of the scene being shot. They were introduced only in the year 2000. So I had to run along with Prakash's camera to actually see the shot through the lens. After we were done, I hugged Prakash with joy. No other cameraperson would have so readily agreed to the experiment.

'It's the first time I've tried out such a shot Prakash,' I said.

'Me too,' he smiled.

I knew it would work out well, just as the masked shot we had attempted for the 'Oru Vennpura' song.

'Let's break for tea,' I announced, amidst laughter and applause.

During the break, I said, 'Such ingenuity shouldn't end abruptly, Prakash. Let's round it off with a stunner.'

'The scene is over. Come on, let's not elongate it,' said Rajni. Shanmugasundaram agreed with him.

But I insisted that the highly-strung character should storm out in style. And that's how we brought in the high-speed shot of Rajni walking out, fast and furious! When Rajni slapped his thigh at those who had betrayed him, turned around dramatically and strode out, the impact was electrifying. The audience's empathy for the underdog who had dared to challenge the rich and mighty was complete!

We needed to shoot a scene where the friends-turned-foes, Annamalai and Ashok, face each other on an escalator. Those were the days when Chennai did not have the device. Mumbai had two. So we went all the way to shoot the scene at the Centaur Hotel in Mumbai. We had obtained permission to shoot at the hotel for eight hours—10 p.m. to 6 a.m. 'Not a minute before or after,' we were told, and I had planned to can at least a dozen shots!

When we landed at the Centaur, a party was going on and several bigwigs of the city were present.

'Sir, the party cannot be disturbed now. Can you shoot after 12,' they asked.

We agreed—not that we had a choice.

At midnight, the hotel management asked us to wait

for some more time, and said we could begin work at 2 a.m.

'In that case, we would like to shoot beyond 6,' we said.

'That's impossible,' was the reply.

We decided to get the lighting done beforehand, but some of the guests at the hotel objected, and we had to beat a hasty retreat.

It was 3 a.m., and the party was showing no signs of winding up. The clock ticked away and finally, at 5 a.m., we were generously told that the place was ours for an hour!

'What can we accomplish in an hour, Suresh? Do you think it's even worth a try,' asked Rajni.

But we had already paid for the shoot, and the entire unit had travelled to Mumbai for the purpose. To organise such a trip all over again would be an arduous task that involved a lot of money. So I said, 'Let's see what we can do, Sir.'

Prakash quickly began shooting wide angles, close-ups, shift-focus (which is simply the focus of the camera shifting from an actor near the camera to another further away) and shots of Rajni snapping his fingers at his arch rivals.

The shift-focus had Sarathbabu and Radha Ravi way down on the escalator. Rajni was made to stand in the foreground. In the earlier part of the film, as a milkman, a commoner, Rajni had slapped his thigh to reinforce the seriousness of his challenge, but the suave and sophisticated businessman of the present had to restrict himself to an effective finger-snapping act.

We then filmed the full key shots or master shots, as they are known. (A master shot is an important element in filming, where all the actors in a scene are in view.) In the scene, you can see Rajni going up the escalator, while Sarathbabu and his father are on their way down. The symbolism was clear—Annamalai's graph was rising, while his enemies' was plummeting. At the end of the scene, Rajni snaps his fingers at his adversaries and delivers his dialogue.

As we were running out of time, I told Prakash to light up the place for the master shots. I instructed Sarath and Radha Ravi to remain in their positions, and had Rajni move to the foreground. It saved time because the lighting didn't have to be altered. The shot from over his shoulder and the snapping of his fingers were filmed in the next five minutes. I then had the camera placed on the ground, and asked Rajni to first go down and then up the escalator again. As the camera whirred, Rajni entered the frame and I had a shot taken when he was half way up. In a fraction of a second I was on the other side of the escalator, beckoning Sarath and Ravi to come closer to the camera and then go down, to give the impression that the two were slowly moving out of the frame. These shots took twenty minutes.

I then directed the camera to move half way down and filmed a shot of Rajni coming up standing sideways and a similar shot of him from the opposite side as it warranted only a minimum change in lighting.

The hotel staff had begun to enter and I knew we had

about two minutes left. Luckily, with great presence of mind, Prakash, even while filming the side shots, had placed the lighting for the opposite angle. The actors quickly took their positions for the final time. We rushed down with the camera and filmed the action, and in the same breath I shouted, 'Pack up!'

The unit was stunned.

'Are you sure this will do?' Rajni kept asking me.

'I am,' I said.

It was all over in just half an hour!

The remaining thirty minutes were required for pack-up, and as promised we were out of the hotel at 6 a.m. An unforgettable race against time!

It was at the editing table that an idea crossed my mind. Instead of having music in the background (re-recording, or RR as it is referred to) for this scene, I thought I would superimpose Rajni's earlier dialogue when, as a milkman, he throws down the gauntlet. Placing the scene that had him speaking vociferously alongside would enhance the impact of the shots on the escalator, I felt. We extended the scene with flash-cuts of the confrontation in a manner that made it completely in sync with the dialogue. For example, at the point Rajni makes caustic comments about his enemies, we inserted close-ups of them.

The most surprising aspect was that the fiery outburst shot earlier and the scene on the escalator filmed much later were almost of the same length so that they could be juxtaposed beautifully! At the exact point Rajni slaps his thigh, we placed the shot of him snapping his fingers and summoning his adversaries to a contest. Tears welled up in my eyes at the perfect synchronisation, which was neither conceived nor shot with such a superimposition in mind!

It is an editor's scene entirely, one that calls for imagination and precision. Even now, every time I watch it, I think of Ganesh and Kumar, the editors. The two talented technicians transported the scene to commendable levels. They had apprenticed under editor N.R. Kittu, and I had known them since my days with KB. Kittu was a technician who had worked with KB and whom the director respected a lot.

Ganesh and Kumar had worked on many of my films, including *Sathya*, my debut. Kumar is no more and Ganesh has now shifted base to the small screen.

When Rajni saw the final edit of the scene, he was thrilled. 'I think you did the shooting and the editing simultaneously in your head,' he laughed and patted me on my back.

Epithets such as extempore and impromptu best describe the way in which *Annamalai* took off, progressed without a hitch, came out and eventually won! Begun without a concrete storyline, the film was shot without a break! And its story and screenplay were developed and improvised on the sets! That it went on to create records at the turnstiles, running for 175 days at a stretch, was nothing short of a miracle! Also, if the hurriedly conceived and executed scenes of the 1992 film are still being talked about it can only be because *Annamalai* was destined to find a slot in Rajni's ever-remembered repertoire of hits.

'*Annamalai* showcased Rajni as an embodiment of heroism. Can it ever be surpassed even by the same twosome,' was a poser that made the rounds then.

The reply to it was, *Baasha*.

II

MAKING A POINT

Cows chewing cud, calves frolicking about, fodder strewn all over the place and their owner milking the animals, oblivious to the mess around him—all these happen in the posh drawing room of a rich politician's home! It was the incongruity of the ambience that was the USP of the much talked-about confrontation scene between the milkman and the local Member of the Legislative Assembly (MLA) in *Annamalai*.

When *Annamalai* was being made, Tamil Nadu was abuzz with rumours about Rajni's political inclinations. Will he or won't he take the plunge, was a question being debated upon, on podia, big and small. From the fan on the street to those in the seat of power, everyone was curious. And naturally the dialogue in his films was keenly monitored for the slightest indication of his decision. Be it an innocuous observation or a fiery comment, it was enough to trigger a whole lot of inferences. So much so, people found innuendos where none existed, and read more into messages that were actually meant only for characters in the film! Against this background, you can well imagine the interest that the scene of Annamalai's war of words with the local MLA kindled.

Annamalai is returning home and his mother and sister run towards him crying out that encroachers are building huts on their land. 'We tried stopping them but it's no use,' the mother moans. Annamalai walks up to the men and politely tells them that the place belongs to him and that it is illegal for them to enter it.

'Lodge a complaint anywhere you wish. Our MLA has told us to occupy this piece of land,' is their reply.

Annamalai shrugs his shoulders with seeming helplessness. 'All right, then. What can I do?' he says, and walks away.

His mother is shocked. 'What do you mean by nodding your head and beating a retreat? It's our property.'

'I asked them, Ma. But they refuse to move,' he says, even as his mother gapes at him, bewildered.

The scene closes at this point . . .

The next scene is at the MLA's house. Vinu Chakravarthy, as Ekaambaram, the MLA, is seated in front of his dressing table with his crony standing behind him.

Looking immensely pleased, he begins to freshen

himself up with body spray, when he hears the sound of cows mooing very near him! Shocked, he gets up, looks down at the hall below and stands transfixed! The sight is nauseating! Wrinkling his nose in disgust, he warns Annamalai, who is casually moving around with his cows in the hall, of dire consequences if he does not remove the animals immediately. The anger in Annamalai's retort turns into a veiled threat.

We knew the scene would draw much attention. Shanmugasundaram wrote the dialogue for it twice, but both versions were found wanting. Suddenly Rajni suggested, 'Why don't we ask KB to write this scene for us?'

Without wasting time, Rajnikanth, Shanmugasundaram and I went over to KB's house.

'This is a scene you have to write,' Rajni requested.

'Why da? You people are managing fine,' replied KB.

'It's a powerful scene. Emotions play a vital part, because it is going to cause a change of heart in the MLA. But it shouldn't be misconstrued as a personal attack on politicians. Only you can do it,' Rajni explained, and KB agreed.

Once KB had written the dialogue for the scene, he called us over to his place. It went thus: 'You people condescend to meet us only before an election when you come to our doorsteps canvassing for votes, after which you disappear for the next five years. But simple folks like me remain the same. I go about my chores, causing no trouble to anyone. Don't make me lose my calm . . .'

We read the lines and found them perfect. They had the typical KB sting. And, of course, Rajni delivered it in style. The whole scene was a single shot without cuts, and Rajni came up with a sterling performance.

The comments of Janakaraj, who accompanies Rajni to the MLA's house, enhanced the impact. It was the time Janakaraj was making a name for himself as a comedian and a character actor, and was busy working in a plethora of films. Today, he has settled down comfortably in the U.S. with his son.

Fight sequences involving Rajni never fail to evoke a positive response—the action that precedes his exchange with Vinu Chakravarthy, is an example.

At the politician's home, Raju Master, our stunt choreographer, had his henchmen surround Rajni, Janakaraj and the cows. Rajni executed the action himself without a double. In those days we didn't have ropes to help heroes jump, kick the enemy and somersault in the air, so fights were filmed after plenty of rehearsals—the balancing act, when Rajni held on to the fighters seemingly to attack them, was actually meant to help him when he jumped or turned over.

Rajni lends uniqueness to his fights with myriad facial expressions that are a mix of the serious and the comical. And these come with an air of invincibility that viewers watching Rajni in action also enjoy the mélange of comic gestures in equal measure. No wonder children go gaga over the Superstar's action sequences. His charisma works wonderfully with them, and if children unanimously love to imitate his body language and style, you have to give it to the man—he knows how to blend effervescence and vibrancy with agility and style. I still remember watching audiences screaming with joy during the opening scenes of *Annamalai*, when the boy playing the young Rajni imitates the Superstar's mannerisms in the fight he has with Sarathbabu junior. In fact, we selected the boy from the group that came to audition for the role mainly because he was able to ape Rajni's style and expressions well.

In between the action, Rajni would bring in his own interjections to enliven the scene; '*Lakshmi, thallu,*' ('Lakshmi, move') was just one of them.

Lakshmi is the name of his cow. As he's fighting the politician's henchmen, it inadvertently comes between them, and Rajni utters the words. As if on cue the creature actually gives way! At the cinemas, viewers smiled because to them, it also showed the bonding between Annamalai and his cows. With Rajni, such improvisations are quite common.

As everything about the sequence was fresh and visually very different, to this day it remains evergreen both for the Superstar's audience and me . . .

Initially, the scene was conceived only as a heated exchange between Annamalai and the MLA. After we had filmed the previous scene, which had people putting up shelters on Annamalai's land and daring him to vacate them, we had a two-day break. We had assembled at Raghavendra Kalyana Mandapam, the wedding hall which belongs to Rajni, to prepare for the next few scenes, when I told him, 'Frankly I'm not too happy with the way your scene with the MLA has been visualised. I feel something is missing.'

'You're right. It doesn't have the essential punch, particularly when it is going to be Annamalai's retaliation for the injustice done to him,' Rajni agreed. 'But how do we make it more spirited?'

'We can bring in some innovations in the fight, but again, shouldn't there be more than just that?'

The brainstorming session gained momentum and members of the crew came up with various ideas. Finally, Natraj looked at Rajni and, thinking aloud, said, 'On the behest of the MLA the men have occupied your cattle shed. Now where will the cattle go? Logically, it should be to his place, shouldn't it?'

I sat up excited. 'Superb!' I shouted. 'We'll take the hero's cattle to the MLA's house!'

Then we tweaked the scene further and gave it a final shape.

I always maintain that new ideas happen only when people sit together and think aloud. I'm often reminded of the incident, which I've heard triggered the invention of the Walkman. The chief of the audio firm and his childhood friend were engrossed in the music they were listening to from a spool of tape playing in front of them. The friend realised that it was time for him to leave. 'I wish I could take the music with me,' he said. The casual comment led the chief to spur his research team on to create a device that would enable people to carry their music with them. The result was the ubiquitous Walkman!

Working together for the betterment of a scene is on similar lines; one idea leads to another and an excellent final draft is arrived at. The director shouldn't construe it as interference. Ego ought not to have a role at all. The team should work in tandem towards a common purpose. No point in each travelling tangentially!

Janakaraj's humorous asides in the course of the fight between Annamalai and the MLA's men were again the result of our brainstorming sessions.

I vividly remember the problems we faced before the release of *Annamalai*. At that point, the political scenario wasn't quite favourable to Rajni. The escalating tension resulted in a new rule being implemented, according to which posters of films were prohibited in the city. The publicity blitzkrieg of the present day was unheard of then. Even the hoarding culture hadn't quite caught on. So, but for an ad in the Tamil daily *Dhina Thanthi*, *Annamalai* had to come out with virtually zero publicity!

Luckily for us, the lack of promos only increased the hype and worked greatly to the film's advantage.

12

UNIQUE TOUCHES

I n the early stages of his career, Amitabh Bachchan
was projected as an angry young man in film after
film. It was director Manmohan Desai who first tapped
his talent for comedy in films such as *Amar Akbar Anthony*
(1977) and *Naseeb* (1981). Again, it was a song like 'My
Name is Antony Gonsalves' (*Amar Akbar Anthony*), which
showed moviegoers that the tall and lanky hero was a
good dancer too. I'm sure it must have been a revelation
to the Big B himself!

Similarly, after films such as *Thillu Mullu*, Rajnikanth's
talent for comedy was wonderfully showcased by writer
Panchu Arunachalam and director S.P. Muthuraman in
Thambikku Endha Ooru (1984). As far as comedic timing
goes, Rajnikanth is a natural.

The job of moulding an actor into an engaging
entertainer rests with the director. Even a thoroughbred
horse needs a capable jockey to spur him on to the winning
post. Rajni is a spontaneous actor, who, when given

challenging situations, is sure to deliver. Also his yen for storytelling makes him come up with some very relevant suggestions. In *Annamalai*, the extension of the scene where he walks out murmuring '*Kadavule, Kadavule*,' (I've discussed the scene in an earlier chapter) after seeing a petrified Khushboo rushing out from her bath, is repeated when Sarathbabu meets her for the first time, in the presence of Rajni.

'Shall I begin with a shocked look, and repeat "*Kadavule, Kadavule*" the moment I see Khush again, as if I'm still in a stupor," Rajni asked me.

'Sure, it should be really funny,' I said. My penchant for comedy helped me visualise the scope such an exclamation would offer. Interesting inputs from the writer and actor are vital to make the fun element work.

Again there's this scene where Rajni hides behind the sofa in Sarathbabu's room on seeing the latter enter with Rekha, the girl he's in love with. He begins to sneeze uncontrollably when her braid that hangs down from the sofa tickles his nostrils. The continuous sneezing and hilarious facial contortions were Rajni's improvisations.

Go back to the scene and you are bound to have a hearty laugh all over again!

Annamalai has an interesting fight sequence that melds romance and comedy. Shooting it was especially enjoyable because Rajni's bytes on the set had everyone around in splits.

It's the first meeting between Annamalai and Subbulakshmi (Khushboo), where he is forced to turn chivalrous and save her from a bunch of hooligans. The sequence had to bring in the sense of a blossoming romance, and include action and humour.

Raju Master had choreographed the stunts in such a way that Rajni had to carry Khushboo in one arm and fight the thugs with the other. Throughout, Rajni had to see to it that none of them touched her. Though brilliantly conceived by Raju, the action was quite a tough proposition for Rajni.

'What do you mean by asking me to lift her with one hand and fight these men with the other? Is it possible? Suresh, you should have got me a slim heroine, I say,' he winked.

Khushboo laughed and said, 'Sir, that's not fair.'

But with his funny comments and asides he made it appear easy.

At the time we were shooting *Annamalai,* Khushboo was practically a cult figure. *Chinna Thambi* (1991), with Prabhu, had already transported her to the pinnacle of popularity. The Rajni–Khushboo pair was the hottest at that time. Yet, both were down-to-earth actors and hence fun and camaraderie permeated the atmosphere. The genial mood made work easy, and Rajni contributed a lot to the levity.

Then Rajni came up with a suggestion. 'I have an idea. Let's try it out. If you think it's fine, we'll do it that way. Initially, I'll concentrate more on my milk cans during the fight. As if, to me, my cans are more important than the woman in my arms.'

It worked really well.

Even today, when I think of the scene, it is Annamalai's bewildered look and concern for the safety of his property, viz., the milk cans, being tossed about during his confrontation with the villains that come to my mind first—even as I write these lines the recollection makes me smile.

The scene where Rajni beats up 'Nizhalgal' Ravi (who played his brother-in-law) was conceived as an emotional outburst of a doting brother, who is unable to tolerate the cruel treatment meted out to his sister (the role was enacted by Vaishnavi). The scene was essential because, in the climax, we had to show Ravi becoming remorseful and turning over a new leaf. Otherwise it would have just been an evitable protraction.

Till then the story travels on a different track, viz., the reversal of roles and fortune, with the milkman turning wealthy and his erstwhile friend, a rich hotelier, finding himself in dire financial straits.

The scene which I'm referring to opens with the ringing of the telephone. Annamalai, who happens to be near the instrument, picks it up. At the other end is his sister. She asks for their mother, but her voice sounds desperate. Sensing her anguish, Annamalai rushes to her house, where he learns that she is being physically abused by her husband.

The scene, as it had been written, seemed dull. I felt it

needed to be pepped up, but it wasn't as though we could do much about it. How could I infuse interest in a scene that involved two people talking over the phone? Finally, I told Rajni, 'Sir, it is an otherwise ordinary scene. But you can make it different. Just act it out in your style. We don't have a strong lead-in for the scene. Your gait and mannerisms should do the trick.'

Rajni laughed out aloud.

'I'm serious, Sir! As a fan I know you can create an impact by the way you act it out.'

For the first time Rajni was at a loss for words. It was as though he had just realised that the director was also his ardent admirer! He looked at me intently for a minute, nodded, and moved to the spot before the camera.

As the camera waited to can the shot, Rajni walked in adjusting the buttons on his jacket, picked up the receiver with a sleight of hand and began talking into it. The movements were intended to showcase the Superstar's style, and the result was stupendous!

We had allotted one day to film the fight sequence between Rajni and 'Nizhalgal' Ravi. The location was Hotel Ambassador Pallava in Chennai. Raju Master had choreographed it as a one-sided fight with Annamalai dominating it. The emotional context behind the scene made it all the more powerful.

The brother-in-law can do nothing but cringe before the picture of puissance towering over him. The scene culminates in Rajni pulling the trigger. The bullets graze past Ravi, who stands shivering in fear. 'Don't you ever think of harming my sister again,' he warns and walks out.

Thanks to Rajni and Raju, the scene turned out to be one of the Superstar's most memorable action segments. At that point in the story, Annamalai isn't an energetic young hero. He is a sedate senior with a different set of challenges to be met. Yet his strength, stamina and style are intact, is the message.

The scene helped boost the post-interval part considerably. Just a two hundred feet long sequence, but the power packed into it made a great difference.

13

UNDERSTANDING THE PHENOMENON

Looking back, I'm shocked at my recklessness. Technicians work on a story for two years or more, polish it over and over again and then begin to transfer their thoughts on to celluloid. But there I was, with a storyline I wasn't too sure about, with which I had to begin shooting in just forty-eight hours, and the hero was Rajnikanth!

I still remember the words of Ramkumar of Sivaji Films, as we stood outside Good Luck (now Four Frames) preview theatre in Nungambakkam, Chennai.

'How could you begin a film in two days, Suresh? I still can't get over it!'

'Faith in the Almighty,' I smiled. 'He takes care of me.'

I remembered saying something similar to KB, after he had watched the double positive of *Annamalai*. (Double positive is the stage when dubbing for a film has been completed and picture and sound are on separate tracks—

a raw copy where visual effects and re-recording remain to be done.) KB had walked up to me and said, 'Are you mad? If I tell you to do something, don't you consider the pros and cons before you accept the proposal?'

I blinked. Was he unhappy with the film?

Seeing my expression he said, 'Okay da, relax, the film has come out well and it is bound to be a hit, but your decision could have spelt disaster for you. Do you realise the risk you've taken? Your career as director could have been in jeopardy if you hadn't been able to pull it off!'

I heaved a sigh of relief. 'The power above is guiding me, Sir,' I had replied.

My debut was in Tamil with the Kamal Haasan film *Sathya* (1988), which turned out to be a blockbuster. *Prema* (1989), my second, was in Telugu, with Venkatesh and Revathi in the lead, and it had had a hundred-day run. Ilaiyaraja was the composer. *Prema* won several awards from the Andhra Pradesh government: Nandi Awards, as they are called, for Best Direction, Best Cinematography (P.S. Prakash), Best Hero and Best Actor in a Supporting Role (S.P. Balasubramaniam). SPB, the popular playback singer, is a commendable actor too.

After *Sathya*, Kamal and I joined hands again for *Indrudu Chandrudu* in Telugu, also in 1989, in which he played a double role. The film ran for a year. It was dubbed in Tamil as *Indran Chandran*, and was a hit all over again. And as Kamal was also popular in Hindi cinema, it was released

Rajnikanth with the famous cycle and the milkman look in *Annamalai*

At the muhurat of *Annamalai*, with (from left) composer Deva, director K. Balachander, executive producer Natrajan, Rajnikanth and cameraman P.S. Prakash

Rajnikanth with dancers during the shooting of the song 'Vandhaenda Paalkaaran' in Ooty

One of the lead scenes in the duet, 'Annamalai, Annamalai, Aasa Vechaen Unnaamala'

Rajnikanth with Crazy Venkatesh in a scene that was deleted from the film in the final footage

Rajnikanth with Janakaraj in the tea shop scene on the sets of *Annamalai*

On the sets of *Annamalai*—a happy family scene before the split. From left, Rekha, Khushboo, Manorama, Vaishnavi, Rajnikanth and Sarathbabu

Annamalai being bribed by a businessman to sell his land

Rajnikanth and Khushboo in the duet, 'Annamalai, Annamalai, Aasa Vechaen Unnaamala'

The lead scene from the famous song 'Kondaiyil Thazhambu, Nenjiley Vazhapoo'

Annamalai takes his cows to the MLA's house and then fights with his cronies

The scene in which Rajnikanth and Khushboo meet in *Annamalai*

The powerful scene in which Rajnikanth angrily tells off the MLA who has taken over his land

Stills from *Veera*

With Rajnikanth, on the sets of *Veera*

Producer Panju Arunachalam (centre) visits the sets during the shooting of the song 'Malaikkovil Vaasalil ...'. Also in the photograph are (from left) dance master Raghuram, Rajnikanth and cameraman P.S. Prakash

My wife and assistant director Chandra with Meena at the outdoor shoot at Talakonna, near Tirupati, during the shooting of the song, 'Maadathilae Kanni Maadathilae'

With the lead pair, Rajnikanth and Meena, at the same outdoor shooting of 'Maadathilae Kanni Maadathilae'

On the sets with cameraman P.S. Prakash

With Senthil and Rajnikanth, shooting a comedy scene

Stills from *Baasha*

Rehearsing the scene where Rajni is tied to a lamp post and beaten. From left, Rajnikanth, associate director Rajeev Prasad, and Anand Raj, who played the villain

Rajnikanth and Nagma, on the massive set that was built at Vijaya Vahuini Studios

Actor Kamal Haasan, who was shooting on a set nearby, visited us to wish us good luck

Rehearsing a scene with Janakaraj and Rajnikanth in the auto-rickshaw stand

Rajni seated on top of a crane for a shot in the song 'Naan Autokaaran'

This is especially for his fans—the famous Rajni Hai

A shot from the 'Style Style' number

The introduction of Rajnikanth as Baasha, shot in Hyderabad

Rajnikanth in one of the many costumes he wore for the 'Nee Nadandha Nadai Azhagu' song

Rajnikanth dressed as a Brahmin priest for the same song, with Nagma

Shots from the 'Naan Autokaaran' song, which became an anthem for auto-rickshaw drivers

Rajnikanth as Baasha in the song 'Ra Ra Raamiah! Ettukkulae Ulagam Irukku Paaraiyya'

The famous introduction scene of Baasha—an electrifying performance

in the north as *Mayor Saab*. Meanwhile, I had made a mark in another Tamil film, *Raja Kaiya Vechcha* (1991). Prabhu, Gauthami and Revathi comprised the main cast. A thorough entertainer with a scintillating score from Ilaiyaraja, it was a decent grosser. *Raja Kaiya Vechcha* would have done even better if it had not been released along with three other films that had Prabhu as the hero.

Thus I had tasted success on a large scale even before I joined hands with Rajnikanth. But it didn't make me lose sight of the fact that directing a Rajnikanth film is a different ball game altogether. He is an actor who transcends the demarcation of A, B and C centres of viewership that the film industry talks about, based on the taste of the audiences in cities, towns and villages. But town or city, educated or illiterate, young or old, Rajnikanth is one actor who touches every filmgoer. Jumping from the bandwagon of Kamal Haasan to that of Rajnikanth and making a mega hit of my first film with him was a giant leap in my career! And thanks to his fans, I had a taste of the star's power soon after the release of *Annamalai*.

I was theatre-hopping in Tiruchi to gauge viewers' responses to *Annamalai*. I wasn't a known face, though my name was familiar to filmgoers. I was standing in a corner with my wife, waiting to watch the audience's reactions to the film, when suddenly the crowd recognised me. It was obvious that they were thrilled to see me there. For them, it was as if Rajnikanth himself was standing amidst them! Thoroughly excited, they carried me on their shoulders all the way from the gates of the cinema to the hall!

Mena Preview Theatre. Rajni, and a few of us who had watched the first copy of *Annamalai* with him, walked out slowly. (First copy—also referred to as 'married print', as picture and sound are together in this version—is the final picture. These days, with the advent of Avid editing and digitised advancements, the first copy can be secured in no time.)

Suddenly Rajni turned around and gave me a hug. 'What a film, Suresh!' he smiled.

As is his wont, he hadn't been present for the editing or the re-recording. So it was the first time he had watched the film in full. Earlier, we had only screened the song sequences for him. Even then he had been very impressed with the way I had shot the fiery number, 'Vetri Nichayam, Idhu Veda Sathiyam'. ('A decisive victory awaits you, It's a promise as true as the Vedas'.)

While shooting at Sea Rock Hotel in Mumbai, which was the location for some of the significant scenes in *Annamalai,* I kept filming random shots of him, asking him to walk from one point to another in his typical style.

'What's the purpose, Suresh?' he asked me.

'They could come in handy later,' I told him. And they did, in the song sequence!

Praising a technician when his work warrants it is an admirable trait in Rajni. Not many heroes have the heart to do so. He knows that such words of encouragement boost the morale of the person and urge him to do better. He has never failed to appreciate my direction when a particular scene impacted him.

This is the right juncture for me to tell you about my wife Chandra. We got married soon after my first film *Sathya* was released. I've always worked in films in various languages. So I would do a Telugu film, go over to a Kannada project and move on to Malayalam, Hindi and so on. Even now it is so. Hence I'm always travelling. And everywhere I go I have a new set of assistants working for me, because there are times when work has to go on simultaneously in two or more languages.

I needed a person to coordinate work in the various areas, and Chandra filled the bill. She was academically oriented, winning medals all her way through college. So cinema was new to her, yet she grasped things quickly, took charge of the dubbing of my films, and was also present on the sets to assist me. So much so, at times Rajnikanth would look at her for approval of a take before turning towards me! And basically, Chandra is a frank person. If she found a shot wanting, she would tell Rajnikanth so, and he would agree with a smile. She knows the pulse of the masses because she is herself a hard-core Rajni fan. If I tried to lend a touch of subtlety or bring in too much finesse, she would tell me, 'No, this won't sell.'

14

BONDING WITH
THE SUPERSTAR

As I told you earlier, *Annamalai* was my first film with Rajni.

Looking back, I realise there was not a single day when the Superstar was haughty or supercilious, throwing tantrums or acting uppity. He treated me with respect and showed genuine affection and warmth that I could work without tension. The atmosphere on the sets was absolutely hassle-free, and the comfort level was so high that it brought out the best in me. Shooting with Rajni was sheer joy. Many a time I would forget that I was the helmsman and begin to enjoy his every movement and nuance before the camera!

The blossoming of a sincere friendship was a natural outcome of our professional compatibility. Soon we began sharing views on various subjects, which led to a bond that continues to be strong to this day. Those two-and-a-half months of interaction were a rewarding period of my life. We travelled to Ooty and Bangalore for work and spent a lot of time together during those trips. In Chennai, we would have casual meetings at his marriage hall, Raghavendra Kalyana Mandapam. We would chat for long hours over the phone, and there were days when he would call me over to his home for lunch.

We shared such positive vibes that, after a point, he just had to begin voicing an idea and I would understand what he was driving at! The telepathy surprised me! And the days remain vivid in my memory. This nostalgic journey to my Rajni days is invigorating indeed . . .

*A*nnamalai was the first film to flash the word 'Superstar' before Rajni's name on screen. Till date the design and the music we introduced precede Rajni's name in the titles of his films.

The film was nearing completion. Shooting had been wrapped up, editing was going on and we were about to begin RR (re-recording). I had a gut feeling that the film would catapult Rajni to the acme of stardom.

Even today, the opening music and the silhouette that are distinctive of films in the James Bond franchise, bowl me over. Surely Rajnikanth, who was becoming a phenomenon, warranted a unique logo to go with his name, I thought. I broached the subject that had been brewing in my mind for a while.

'Sir, the opportunity to work with you in these three months of shooting has only increased my liking for you.

And out there, are innumerable admirers, who may not know Rajni the person, but who are still equally captivated by your screen presence. Your charisma is such. Till now you've been described as the Superstar by a few. But the time has come for the status to precede your name in the titles. So I'll create a logo and a signature tune for it, which will announce the arrival of Brand Rajni. The impact will be magical,' I said.

'Don't be ridiculous, Suresh! I can't allow such brazen self-aggrandisement. It's embarrassing,' he rejected my suggestion outright. That only showed the humility of Rajni.

But I wasn't going to give up because I knew his fans would love it. The next time I met KB, I told him about our conversation and Rajni's reluctance. 'We ought to have it, Sir! The response should be amazing.'

KB liked the idea and called up Rajni at once.

'What's your problem, Rajni? Why do you object to it? You *are* a superstar! What's wrong with saying it? I think Suresh has a point. We are going ahead and prefixing it to your name.' And that was it.

Graphics was in its nascent stage then, but the boys enthusiastically brought in lights to shine on each alphabet of 'SUPERSTAR', and followed it up with the name 'RAJNI' emerging from it, all in huge, bold lettering.

Once the logo was ready, we sat down for RR as I had decided we needed music that would be the signature tune for all Rajni films. At the composing studio, I said, 'The moment the music begins, viewers should recognise it as a Superstar film, Deva. Have you noticed the background score in Hollywood war films? The melody is unique and the reverberating beats are like a clarion call for battle. Can you try something on those lines?'

Deva, who loves trying out new ideas, enthusiastically sat down to compose a wonderful theme piece and interspersed it with resounding shouts of, 'Hey! Hey!' to match the rhythm of the beats. The tune caught on instantly and everyone in the studio—Deva's brothers and assistants, Sabesh and Murali, who are a great support to him and are equally talented, the musicians and sound engineers—all began to walk towards the voice room snapping their fingers and shouting 'Hey! Hey!'

'Super!' was the unanimous response.

And I saw it as a precursor to the reaction it was going to evoke at the cinemas.

I was so thrilled with the music, that I used the 'Hey! Hey!' and the beats at all the significant junctures of *Annamalai*. Even today the magic of the theme music and the mood of revelry it creates remain unsurpassed!

The opening day of *Annamalai*. Albert Theatre. The first show. Even as the alphabet 'S' appeared on screen, the audience began to scream and whistle. Just one letter, but the waves of joy at the theatres were incredible! I still wonder how they knew that the letter 'S' was going to spell the word 'Superstar'! How could such deafening applause begin even before the entire word was flashed? Till now, the reaction remains a mystery to me. Another clear signal that Rajni, the actor, had scaled the zenith of fame!

Rajni heard about it too. 'I don't believe this, Suresh!' he called up to say. 'Is it true that the response to the logo was overwhelming? Now they will expect it in every film, won't they,' he laughed.

Soon 'Baasha' would arrive to further reiterate Rajni's unassailability as a superstar!

After *Baasha*, Rajni moved on to *Muthu* (1995) and followed it up with *Arunachalam* (1997). One morning I got a call from him. 'Can you come over to AVM Studios, Suresh? I'm here,' he said. He had just begun shooting for *Arunachalam* then, and I wasn't its director; C. Sundar was. Why would he wish to see me?

'Do you realise the tension you have caused me?' His poser as I was walking towards him caught me off-guard.

'What have I done?'

'What more could you have done? You've boosted my image to such an extent that I have to constantly put up a valorous front on screen. You've made me look invincible. The "Hey! Hey!" beats in one and the echoes of "Baasha! Baasha!" in the other have woven a magic spell! Now the makers and the audiences want me to match the same kind of heroism in every film. Earlier, if I had four men walking behind me to show that I'm powerful and infallible, now I'm forced to have a hundred! It's all your doing, Suresh!'

For a minute I thought he was serious. 'I am,' he said, as if reading my thoughts. But I broke into a fit of laughter—laughter born out of the satisfaction that I had placed the Superstar on a pedestal so high that it was a challenge for others to meet it! If *Annamalai* and *Baasha* are being seen as trendsetters, nothing can give me more joy!

'It is three years since *Baasha*. I've done *Muthu* after it. But people are still in the grip of *Baasha*. How can I go on exuding such heroism in film after film? Whatever I do doesn't seem enough.'

He sounded genuine, but I couldn't conceal my happiness. He was quiet for a while. And I slowly asked, 'What else, Sir?'

'That's all. I wanted to convey my suffering to you in person. I've done it and I feel better.' This time he joined me in the laughter!

After the release of *Annamalai*, Rajni organised a projection of the film for Sivaji Ganesan. I had never met the thespian earlier. Thanks to Rajni, I got the opportunity. Sivaji Ganesan's sons Ramkumar and Prabhu had accompanied him. After the show, he came out and spoke to Rajni, while I stood a little away from them. Rajni looked around, called me over and introduced me to the veteran. He patted my cheek like he would a child's and said, 'In my heyday, the camera remained steady while I would move up and down to make an impact as a hero, but you've limited Rajni's movements and made the camera whirl around. The dynamism of the shots have helped project heroism better. Great job, son! You've showcased another dimension of Rajni. The film's plus is its making. It's surely going to be a hit!' I was overwhelmed.

The great actor's encouraging words and his prophecy still ring in my ears . . .

15

ON A RELUCTANT NOTE

Rajnikanth and I had just finished watching the Telugu film *Allari Mogadu*, directed by Raghavendra Rao, with Mohan Babu as hero.

'How do you like the film, Suresh?' Rajni asked me as we were walking out. Before I could reply, he continued, 'I think we should remake it in Tamil.'

I was taken aback.

'Are you kidding, Sir?'

After *Annamalai*'s massive run, Rajni had come out with *Pandian* in the same year, which didn't work much at the box office. *Valli* (1993), his home production, which K. Natraj had directed, and Rajni himself had scripted, and *Uzhaippaali*, again in the same year, had also been released.

His films were being released at regular intervals, yet Rajni's overpowering charisma as Annamalai still seemed to hold filmgoers in a strong grip. The magic created by *Annamalai* seemed irreplaceable!

Meanwhile, though Rajni was busy, he would often call me over for a chat. We would watch his other films and in the course of our conversation he would remark, 'The audiences want us to come back again, Suresh. I'm thinking about it seriously.' I would smile and leave it at that, knowing well that he would give me the assignment at the appropriate time. And as we had already talked about it, I assumed our next film together would be *Baasha*. Rajni had decided on the title and we had even discussed a few scenes.

So when he invited me over to his place and said, 'We'll be doing a film for Panchu Arunachalam. And we are watching a Telugu film today,' I was slightly confused. As I said, I was under the impression that *Baasha* would be our second project together. I just nodded and accompanied him to the film. It was *Allari Mogadu*. I watched it with an open mind—I thought he only wanted me to catch up with his friend Mohan Babu's latest release.

But when, after the show, he said we should team up for the remake of it, I was shocked!

'I'm serious, Suresh! It'll work,' he smiled.

I looked around; Panchu Arunachalam and the others who had sat through the show with us appeared equally happy. How could they even think that we could make a winner out of this? It was the story of a hero, with two wives. A typical commercial film made to cater for a mass audience! The values associated with a Rajni starrer were completely missing. The double entendres in *Allari Mogadu* could never be allowed in a Rajni film because his fan base comprises the rustic and the urbane, the elite and the mass, the young and the old. And why a Telugu remake at all, particularly after a grand success called *Annamalai*? I was puzzled.

'Sir, you cannot star in a role that shows you with two wives. Your audience will not accept bigamy from a hero like you. According to them, you can do no wrong,' I began.

'It is a runaway hit in Andhra Pradesh, Suresh. We can make a few changes to suit the Tamil audience,' Rajni said, and the others, including Panchu Arunachalam, nodded.

'Sir, why don't we go with *Baasha*? You sounded very enthusiastic about it, remember?'

'Of course, we'll do it. But not now,' he said, and I could argue no further.

Nevertheless my conscience didn't allow me to accept the film without making an earnest attempt to dissuade him from the idea. 'I'll jot down my counters on a piece of paper and hand it over to him before he makes a final decision,' I told myself and began to write out the positives and the negatives on a sheet of foolscap paper, for his consideration . . .

Besides the doubts I had already raised in person, I added that the film offers no scope for heroism; that action is completely missing; and that a strong villain is nowhere in the picture. My last statement was that, after a phenomenal hit, did we need to go in for a subject that was rather crude?

When I met him next, I handed the sheet over to him saying, 'Don't mistake me, Sir. Honestly, I thought I should place all the cards on the table. If you still wish to go ahead, I'm game,' I smiled.

Rajni guffawed in his typical style. 'Listen Suresh,' he began in a placating tone, and explained his point patiently. 'It's obvious that my fans haven't forgotten *Annamalai*, so our second film together is bound to be compared to it. And even if we fill it to the brim with heroic action, they might still compare it with *Annamalai* and find it wanting. But if we shift the focus, give them a different kind of subject and later return to the action genre, the impact will be more. And even if they compare our second with the first, they won't be disappointed because this will be in a completely different league, dealing with love, comedy and sentiment.'

His strategy seemed sound, but I was still hesitant.

'Don't you find any redeeming feature in the film?' he said, keen that I enter the project wholeheartedly.

'Of course I do. I think the comedy angle will work in Tamil too,' I told him. 'But everything has to be altered to a great extent.'

'Well, then go ahead and alter it. We'll change the segments that you feel have to be corrected.'

His words gave me hope. If we reworked the script drastically, we could have a hit, I thought.

A man falls in love with a girl and gets married to her at a temple. A grand wedding will follow in the presence of their kith and kin, they promise each other. But before their plan is realised, tragedy strikes. The girl dies, or so everyone thinks. The shattered hero leaves his village and goes to the city, where he meets another girl, who shows him the way to a bright career as a singer. She falls in love with him and circumstances make them husband and wife. Just as he slowly reconciles himself to the loss of the woman he was deeply in love with and begins to reciprocate the feelings of the new girl in his life, the first wife returns . . .

'We'll justify the hero's decisions with a blend of humour. We'll bring in a villain who is obsessed with the girl he meets in the city. We'll make the mother of the hero a strong character. It is because of her insistence that he agrees to marry again . . .' I went on. Slowly, I began to believe that we could borrow just the basic storyline and transform it into a film suitable for Rajni's image and audience's taste.

Taj Banjara in Hyderabad is Rajni's favourite spot. So off we went to discuss the plot threadbare and reach a consensus about the story. Soon we had a fresh outline ready. The job took us ten days.

Once we returned to Chennai, we met Panchu Arunachalam and gave him the final draft of the story. Panchu is one of the finest screenplay writers I've come across. He made suggestions about the segments that had to be retained and those we could do away with, and substantiated his stand with logical explanations. Slowly my confidence in the project increased.

And thus *Veera* was born . . .

16

BELLING THE CAT

My confidence level was rising all right, yet I continued to remain sceptical about *Veera*. Making the audience accept their matinee idol as a man with two wives was no mean task. Trying to justify his actions was a struggle that gave me sleepless nights. I still maintain that it is the comedy angle we resorted to in the film that worked in our favour. Coupled with it was the Rajni factor—with *Annamalai* his popularity had soared to unimaginable heights. These factors steered *Veera* to victory.

The Telugu original didn't have the emotional profundity of *Veera*. We managed to establish that the hero practised high values in life, and if he had two wives, it was because of circumstances beyond his control. We laid emphasis on the premise that, though changes in his life drove him to another woman, his feelings for his first wife were sincere. He hadn't forgotten her; it was his mother who forced him into marriage again. So the character of the protagonist in *Veera* was very different from his counterpart in *Allari Mogadu*, in which matters of the heart had been handled superficially. Ramya Krishnan played the second wife in Telugu, the role which Roja replicated in Tamil. Meena was common to the two versions—she played the first wife in both.

Character actor Vadivukkarasi played the part of Rajnikanth's mother. She realises that the thread his first wife Meena had tied round her son's wrist, is the bond that deters him from beginning life afresh with Roja. He continues to wear it even after Meena has disappeared. So, the mother wrenches it from his wrist, as if to suggest that the bonding with the first wife has been severed completely, and that he's now free from the shackles of the past, which are bogging him down.

The symbolism in the scene was entirely Panchu Arunachalam's idea and it improved the impact of the narration tremendously. The Telugu version was sans such sentimental touches.

Again, in *Allari Mogadu*, the second wife's desire for Mohan Babu was more on a physical plane. But in *Veera*, the carnal aspect was secondary.

Thus we polished the screenplay over and over again till it gathered sheen. Eventually, but for the basic plot, *Veera* emerged as a near-new product. It was then that I actually felt we were ready to shoot.

The hero is a reluctant husband, still grieving the loss of his first wife (Meena), till one evening he returns home to see an incredibly large image of him drawn on the floor and painstakingly coloured. Looking absolutely diminutive beside it is the artist, his new wife (Roja), lying on the floor exhausted. His heart melts for her, and for the first time since their marriage, he embraces her with genuine love.

The next morning he enters his music studio, feeling happy after a very long time. The recording for the day is over and he walks out casually. In the hall outside is his first wife waiting for him! He sees her under a lone light, and is caught unawares. Shock, joy and dismay dance on his face in turns . . .

Prakash had all the lights save one switched off for the scene. A small circle of light was focused on Meena, who was made to sit in the midst of encircling darkness. The shadow that the light created around her was beautiful.

It was a poignant scene and Prakash had canned it so beautifully that it is still a visual stunner!

In the normal course, the narration ought to have taken a serious turn at this point. But we maintained it as a rip-roaring session all the way.

Maestro Ilaiyaraja's songs and euphonious background score were indisputable value additions of *Veera*. As a connoisseur of music, working with Ilaiyaraja has always been a joyous experience for me. My maiden film, *Sathya*, was with this genius. We followed it up with some wondrous music that he provided for my Telugu films, *Indrudu Chandrudu* (*Indran Chandran* in Tamil) and *Prema*, and *Raja Kaiya Vechcha* in Tamil.

However, for *Annamalai*, I had gone with Deva. Rajni's films after *Annamalai*—*Pandian* and *Uzhaipaali*—had had Ilaiyaraja's score. And for Panchu Arunachalam, it always had to be Ilaiyaraja.

I was meeting Ilaiyaraja for the first time after working with Deva for *Annamalai*. So I wasn't too sure about his reaction on seeing me. But when Panchu said, 'Raja, I think you know Suresh will be directing our film,' his instant response was, 'Of course. We've worked together on several films. I may compose many numbers, but it isn't often that a song such as the 'Valaiyosai' piece in *Sathya* happens. Lata Mangeshkar sang it, remember? Suresh has a taste for music.'

My tension abated and I began discussing the song situations in *Veera* with enthusiasm.

We left for Rajahmundry, in Andhra Pradesh, for the shoot—it was our first location. Meanwhile, Ilaiyaraja had recorded the first duet for the film. It was sent to us at the location for feedback. Strangely, the song didn't quite appeal to me as much as an Ilaiyaraja composition generally does. The tune was wonderful, no doubt, but it didn't quite convey the feeling I'd expected it to. I didn't want to make a hasty decision though, so I played it for Rajni. His reaction was similar to mine. The members of the unit who heard it also told me that it didn't jell with the sequence we had in mind.

Still, I was reluctant to dismiss the composition at once and went back to the song. But even when I listened to it with an open mind over and over again, the only conclusion I could arrive at was, as a song it was brilliant, yet it was not quite apt for the situation I had conceived. Something was missing, though I couldn't put my finger on what it was.

The problem was, Panchu Arunachalam had heard the tune, and only after he'd approved it had the song been recorded. How could we tell a composer of Ilaiyaraja's stature that we want it changed? And who would dare do it? Of course, I was fully aware that as the helmsman it was my responsibility. But how was I going to bring myself to convey my opinion to the maestro?

The thought weighed me down throughout my journey from Rajahmundry to Chennai. I was tense, and could think of nothing else . . .

Ilaiyaraja was at AVM Studios when I went over to meet him. He greeted me with a smile.

'What brings you here so early in the day? Did you listen to the song?'

I had to respond. Wiping the beads of sweat on my forehead I said, 'Yes . . . but . . .'

'Come on, tell me. What is it?'

'It's about the song,' I started, and then, in a hurry, added, 'It's definitely good . . .'

'Then what's the problem?' he asked, looking at me intently. I was sure he was reading my thoughts.

'As I told you, the number per se is great, but the others feel it isn't exactly in tune with the mood of the sequence,' I managed to say.

Ilaiyaraja raised his hand as if to stop me from saying anything further.

'Since when did you begin going by others' opinions? I thought your decisions were your own.'

'It's not like that, Sir. We were all sitting together, listening to the song on the nagara and they reacted to it. . . Still, Raja, if you think it's fine, no problem, we'll retain it—'

Before I could say anything more, he said, 'All right, Suresh,' and picked up the telephone receiver. He dialled Panchu Arunachalam's number. Just as the voice at the other end said, 'Hello,' Ilaiyaraja succinctly stated, 'Your director says he doesn't like my song,' and unceremoniously cut the line.

The next second, he called Rajnikanth. 'Rajni, your director doesn't like my song,' he repeated and placed the receiver in the cradle. I just sat there blinking!

He then turned round to me and said, 'Okay, accept that what you told me is your opinion. Why do you say that others didn't appreciate it? That upsets me, Suresh. And if you don't mind, let's meet later.'

The abruptness and finality in his tone set me thinking of the consequences my plain speaking was going to have.

17

SONG AND SEQUENCE

I came out of AVM Studios and drove straight to Panchu Arunachalam's house. Rajnikanth was already there. Ilaiyaraja's phone call had rattled them.

'What happened, Suresh?' Panchu greeted me with a query that clearly revealed his angst. 'Raja seems quite upset. The song sounded fine to me.'

'Sir, I was just being honest. Don't I know he's a music wizard? All his songs for my films have been hits. Only that I found this particular number slightly unsuitable. If you don't wish to have it changed, I'll retain it. But I thought it was better to have the nagging thought out of my system. You tell me what I should do.'

'I understand your point, Suresh. But how are we going to appease his anger?'

'I think he was just as frank as I was. He wasn't serious, I assure you. I know him Sir,' I said.

But deep inside, I had misgivings. Had Ilaiyaraja taken umbrage? If so, what would be his next step? I wasn't sure. Yet I didn't want Panchu to get worked up further.

Rajnikanth spoke for the first time. 'Under the circumstances, the best option is to wait and watch. Let Raja get back to us. For now, we'll just let the matter rest,' he said.

The suggestion appealed to Panchu and me.

Within a couple of hours, Raja called up the three of us. He said he wanted us to come over to his studio together.

My sigh of relief was almost audible when I saw him welcome me with a broad smile. But it was Rajni who broke the ice. I've always been fascinated by his understanding of the psychology of people. Being very perceptive, he instinctively knows the mood of the person before him and strikes the right chord.

With a broad grin, he said, 'Raja, the problem is, just because you've made the AVM premises your workplace, you give them all the best songs. Can anyone ever dream of composing the fabulous tunes you offered us for AVM's *Ejamaan*? What crime has an ordinary trio like us committed? Agreed, we are comparatively a small producer, director and hero who've come together. But show us some consideration, Raja, ha, ha, ha,' he guffawed.

Ilaiyaraja joined him in the laughter. The camaraderie eased the tension. And as the friendly banter continued, Raja began to look really happy.

He then turned around, glanced at me and told Rajni, 'I know Suresh very well. So I was peeved when he said that others in the unit felt the tune isn't suitable. He could have been more straightforward about it. I would have felt better that way.'

'Let's not go back to it, Raja. You know that Suresh has the utmost regard for your talent,' Rajni mollified him.

'I think I got a hang of what Suresh wants, so I've changed all the tunes that I had originally composed,' he smiled.

And as he played them one after the other, we listened fascinated. Each was a gem. Thus were born the timeless melodies of *Veera*, which are an aural treat to this day.

At the end of the session, Rajni's wit came to the fore once again. 'One thing is clear, Raja. When you get worked up you come up with splendid tunes,' he winked, and the inimitable tunesmith joined him in the chuckle!

I t was decided that 'Maadathilae Kanni Maadathilae', the evergreen hit, would be shot on the lead pair, with forty dancers around them, at Thalakonna, a forest that is an hour's drive from Tirupati. It is a beautiful location with a small temple in the middle of lustrous greenery. All the dancers were to be in traditional Brahmin attire, because, according to the story, the heroine belonged to the community.

We landed at the spot on time. The artistes got ready, and Raghuram, the choreographer, rehearsed the footwork with the dancers. Just when they were about to go for the first shot, I had the uneasy feeling that it wasn't going the way I had envisaged it. The classiness

I'd wanted was missing. In fact, it appeared crude! Was I imagining it, or were others in the unit also feeling the same way? I looked around and noticed my wife, Chandra, and Sundaramurthy, the make-up artist, tittering away. I walked up to them.

'What's so funny?'

'That's how the shot looks,' they chorused. 'And not merely funny, absolutely bad!'

I felt like seconding their opinion aloud, but refrained from doing so. I had just stirred up a hornet's nest about Ilaiyaraja's score, though luckily, it had only helped us get some lovely music out of the maestro. Now if I make an issue about the song sequence after bringing the entire cast and crew outdoors, Rajnikanth may not take it lightly, I thought. At the same time, though, I could not allow this apology of a sequence to go on. 'What do you mean by saying it's no good? We've travelled all the way, had breakfast, and now the artistes are ready with their make-up on. It's too late to suggest changes,' I told them. My voice didn't sound convincing even to me. If I accepted the sequence as it was, not only would it affect me as a director, but also mar the beautiful melody that Ilaiyaraja had given us.

As things looked, I had the foreboding that the entire sequence was all set to turn into an irrevocable spoiler.

'Everything is okay, isn't it Suresh? We'll check out the movements once and go for the take.' I turned round and saw Rajni standing beside me. I gave a half-hearted nod and Rajni went away to take his position in front of the camera.

As I've said, I take a keen interest in song sequences. And as we didn't have monitors in those days, I would plonk myself beside the cameraperson and watch the detailing of the sequences. But this time I couldn't bring myself to go anywhere near the shooting area, let alone the camera. Come hell or high water I had to stop the shoot. But before that, I had to be armed with a suitable alternative. And frankly, I had none. I was just sure the sequence could not be shot the way it was being done, period. But at that moment, I didn't know a way to better it. I needed time to think. I had to convince the Superstar that we were making a mistake. . .

Perspicacious as he is, Rajni noticed me standing far away and called out.

When I came closer, he asked, 'I know something is eating you. What is it, Suresh?'

I looked at him for a second and then said, 'If I point out a problem I should offer a remedy. I can see the snag but I don't have a solution.'

'First tell me the problem,' Rajni urged.

Deciding to come out with it, I took a deep breath and said, 'Sorry, Sir! I don't like the way the sequence is being filmed.'

'But when all of us sat together and discussed it you were quite happy with the idea!' he said, confused.

'Right, Sir. But now I realise the visual feel that has to

go with the melody is missing. It's too garish. This kind of a dance in traditional costume, in an outdoor milieu, looks bizarre, believe me.'

'Do you want us to pack up?' Rajni was shocked.

'What else can we do, Sir? Let's get back to the hotel and think of a way out,' I suggested.

Even as Rajni was looking at me quizzically, ideas began to form in my mind. 'Let's make it a conventional Brahmin wedding sequence, beginning with the groom alighting from the car at the entrance to the mandapam. We'll include all the rituals with the fun, frolic and grandeur that go with it, right up to the first night of the couple and their next morning together,' I said. 'It will be a surrealistic sequence. It's a sweet song, let's make it visually unique.'

I could make out that Rajni was getting hooked to the idea. He called for the crew—the assistants, dance master, art director and cinematographer.

'Suresh isn't happy with the way the sequence is being shot. So let's get back to the hotel and talk about it,' he told them.

In a couple of hours we were back at Hotel Bhimas in Tirupati, where we were staying. The dancers had given us four days for the song, out of which we had already lost one. And Rajni is a very conscientious actor who never allows the producer to suffer. So work had to be completed in the next three days.

'We have to make up for the lost time and effort, Suresh,' he said.

'We'll leave for Chennai right away.'

'All right but once in Chennai, what happens?'

'The house used in Visu's *Samsaaram Adhu Minsaaram* at AVM will be ideal as the home of the newlyweds. We'll paint the pillars and doors in rich copper against a background of black,' I began, and our enthusiastic art director Magie took over. 'I'll have sparkling pots of stainless steel and other utensils arranged one above the other to decorate the setting,' he said, and soon each of the crew members came up with interesting inputs.

'What about the groom's procession, the wedding ceremony? Where do we shoot that?'

At once Rajni called up his marriage hall, Raghavendra Kalyana Mandapam.

'Is the hall free in the next three days?'

'The day after tomorrow hasn't been booked,' said the voice at the other end.

'Block it,' he said.

Once the modalities had been taken care of, Rajni called up Panchu. 'We are returning to Chennai. We have changed our plans about the song sequence as it isn't coming out as we expected,' he said.

'Rajni, whatever you and the director decide is fine with me. I'm confident that you people know what you are doing,' was Panchu's instant response.

The Superstar was moved by Panchu's trust in us. So was I.

18

BEHIND THE FOOTWORK

'Wow!' I told myself when I saw the house at the AVM premises, where we were to shoot the song sequence that morning. Our location for the day glistened in the morning rays of the Sun. Prakash had done a brilliant job of the lighting. The colour tones were awesome. Magie had worked overtime to make the place awesome. Muted and lustrous at once, the props offered a splendid spread.

We began with the shot that had Rajni being given the traditional oil massage prior to the wedding. His reactions on seeing the bride, his mild exasperation at the girls who pull her away from him, the love in his eyes, and the desire—Prakash captured them all exquisitely. And Raghuram's gentle, teasing footwork enhanced the effect.

Later, just a small piece of music remained to be filled up with movements. We found a suitable spot—the lawns of AVM Studios—and made a beeline for it. The entire group was made to sport sunglasses and dance, holding colourful parasols. Raghuram's synchronised steps for the segment, which were akin to an elegant Western dance, made it a visual treat. As I watched 'Maadathilae Kanni Maadathilae' being canned the way I wanted it, I felt completely satisfied. Each shot fell in place flawlessly and I knew that we had a winner of a sequence in our hands.

M y initial disinclination to bring out *Allari Mogadu* in Tamil made me steadfast in my decision that the audience shouldn't be reminded of the Telugu original at any point. The Tamil version had to be very different. Hence I introduced several changes in the script of *Veera*. The result, as I visualised it, appeared promising.

And I was sure that music would prove to be another elevating aspect. These positives made me work with renewed vigour for the next number.

The mellifluousness of the 'Malaikkovil Vaasalil . . .' ('At the entrance to the hill temple') number, with its unusual rhythm segment, warranted special treatment.

In *Veera,* Rajnikanth's name is Muthu. It is only after he comes to the city that he is known as Veera. Meena, his first wife in the film, knows him only as Muthu. So, for the song, I suggested we have the letters 'M-U-T-H-U' in Tamil on the ground, on which the heroine lights several lamps. A top angle shot would highlight the name of the hero, bright in the dark backdrop of the night.

I envisaged something on a very large scale, something

really big. The girl is deeply in love with the hero, and it manifests itself in the mammoth artwork of lights that she creates for him. 'She should appear a mere spot in the middle of gigantic lamps that glow brightly,' I said. And for a five feet and a few inches tall heroine to look like a Lilliputian beside the lights, it meant that each of the lamps had to be at least three hundred feet high!

The idea was fascinating, but how feasible was it?

'In that case I need much greater height for me to position the camera and shoot,' Prakash contended. We didn't have jimmy jib or Akela cranes in those days to capture such a mind-boggling canvas.

Scouting for the right location for the sequence took quite a while. Finally we zeroed in on the MRF racing track at Sriperumbudur, near Chennai. But the winds blowing at a high velocity in the vast open space made it impossible to keep the candles burning. We experimented for days on end. Finally we tried it out successfully with chimney lamps that blocked the wind from extinguishing the lights.

The number of lamps that had to glow simultaneously was twenty thousand! Today graphics can help you get the effect in a jiffy, but in 1994, each lamp had to be lit physically and kept burning till the completion of the shot.

Prakash perched himself high up on the tower near the track, about two hundred feet away from the actual spot, so that his camera could zoom in and out for best results.

Another trying part was the lettering. The word 'M-U-T-H-U' had to be written on the ground properly, so that when the lamps on them were lit, each letter would stand out distinctly. When viewed through the lens it had to be picture perfect. So, as the letters were being drawn on the ground far away by the art director's men, instructions were given from high above, viz., the tower. We formed a human chain of sorts and kept passing messages from one to the other, without much loss of time. The men worked from dawn to dusk to complete the letters and light the candles. Only when the task was accomplished did the magnitude of the effort sink in!

We went for the take that night. Rajni was made to stand in the foreground and when Meena went and stood amongst the lamps, she was a minute spot in the exquisite play of light and darkness.

'Malaikkovil Vaasalil' has been one of the most strenuous and painstakingly shot sequences in my career.

When Rajni entered the racing track for the sequence that evening, he didn't quite understand the kind of toil that had gone into it. 'You just had to write out the word "Muthu" and light up the candles. I don't quite follow. Why should it have been so difficult,' he asked.

But once I took him up the tower and showed him the entire expanse of land that was used, the number of candles and how they were placed, he was awe-struck.

'Mind-blowing effort, Suresh,' he commended. He congratulated Magie and his entire team, and as a token of his appreciation, he gifted them with cash! Then turning to me, he chortled, 'Suresh, if a girl shows her love for me in this manner, I'll surely fall for her, ha, ha, ha!' I joined him in the laughter.

As a sequence, the 'Konji Konji Malargalaada' ('The flowers sway caressingly') solo sung by S.P. Balasubramaniam didn't offer scope for much innovation. It was a song rendered on stage by the hero, as he played on the harmonium, with his friend and assistant on the tabla. Popular comedian Senthil acted in the role of the accompanist. It was filmed at Narada Gana Sabha, in Chennai.

The song was an aural treat all right, but visually it didn't lend itself to anything very vibrant. So I split the song into four parts, and inserted scenes where Roja visualises Rajni in various outfits and begins to find him very attractive. No romantic dance was involved. It was Rajni's style and gestures that made the segment come alive.

I had a reason for filming it so. Till then we'd showed Rajni, who is in the city, dressed in simple black trousers and a white shirt. So I thought that this was a chance to showcase him in a variety of costumes, along with his stylish mannerisms.

Also, according to the screenplay, there would be a

change in his attire and appearance only in the latter half of the film. 'Let the audience get a glimpse of how he would look later on in the film,' I thought. I was very satisfied with the way we conceived and executed the sequence.

Raghuram was a favourite choreographer of mine. Our association began during the days of *Ek Duuje Ke Liye*, when I worked under KB—Raghuram was the choreographer in nearly all his films. Apart from *Annamalai*, where Prabhu Deva had the cast dance to his tune, I always went with Raghuram, right from *Sathya* to *Sangamam*, till he decided to retire from cinema.

One of the advantages of working with Raghuram was that he was also technically knowledgeable. He was adept at shot placements because he was a director himself. We shared excellent vibes and I still miss him while working in the song and dance segments of my films.

19

SERIOUSLY FUNNY

In the previous chapter, I had mentioned the significance of floor drawings in *Veera*. The letters of the name MUTHU were actually drawn carefully on the ground, as though it were a picture, I had said. Another drawing that involved immense talent and zeal was the creation of an incredibly large, multi-hued kolam, or rangoli, of Rajni—a work so huge that it covered a floor area of 100 x 200 feet—shown in the film as Roja's work of art that underlines her love for her husband.

Among Magie's assistants, Mani was the only artist adept at the art of kolam. But how could he possibly work on the massive illustration without placing his feet on it? It had to be first sketched and then filled in with coloured powder.

After much deliberation and discussion, we had a long rope attached to a pulley, one side of which was tied to Mani's waist. He was then made to hang horizontally from it, with his face and hands turned towards the floor, and complete the task. The contraption worked beautifully and Mani went about his job with gusto. It took him all of two days and two nights! Every now and then he would be pulled higher, for him to get a top angle view of his work, so that he could make essential changes and gauge whether the effort was yielding proper results.

Slowly, right in front of our eyes, an awesome piece of art emerged.

Even as Mani was giving finishing touches to the colouring, I instructed the others in the unit to protect it with utmost care. None should be allowed to stray into the area till the shoot was over, as re-working on it could be well-nigh impossible, I cautioned.

Later, when I entered the floor for shooting, I still found the kolam left unguarded. 'Will someone place a sturdy rope around it so that nobody thinks it is a painted piece which has dried up, and treads on it carelessly?' I called out again.

'We are all here, Sir, don't worry,' the men around assured me.

I went over to the other side of the floor to discuss the scene with my assistants. As I walked past, I noticed a couple of outsiders walking towards the area and told them to move away. Then I turned around to my men and exhorted them once again, 'Please do as I say. Place a rope around it.'

But they didn't quite comprehend my anxiety. I had watched Mani slogging it out, hanging from a rope, for forty-eight hours; I couldn't allow negligence to spoil the output even slightly.

Rajni walked in. Seeing a colourful replica of himself staring at him from the floor, he took a step backward in surprise.

'Wonderful,' he said. 'How did the artist manage to do it?'

I began explaining the process, the use of the rope and pulley, and the position from which Mani dangled to draw it. We were absorbed in the conversation, when I casually turned and saw a fan rushing straight through the middle of the gigantic kolam to meet Rajni! I was aghast!

Probably for the first time in my career as director I hollered out on the set! 'Stop that man! Look at the damage he's done! How long have I been telling you folks to guard the area? You didn't think it was important, and now see what has happened! Now, all of you stop staring at me and do something about it, and do it fast,' I screamed at the top of my voice, and the set that had about fifty people froze into silence. It became so quiet, you could hear a pin drop!

I regained composure and looked around. Everyone began running helter-skelter for ropes, planks and other stuff to barricade the place.

And as I slowly turned towards Rajni, I noticed him watching me with a mischievous smile on his face.

'What's so funny, Sir?' I grinned sheepishly and continued, 'How could they be so careless? I know the extent of hard work that has gone into it. If only they had paid heed to my words . . .'

I thought his response would be, 'Your anger is completely justified, Suresh.'

Instead, he said, 'I'm happy, Suresh, very happy. From the time I've known you, there were days when I would wonder whether you are superhuman, because you've always been unbelievably calm and composed. I've never seen you getting worked up about anything. Your equanimity has been amazing. Now this reaction is something I'm seeing for the first time. Thank you Suresh, for showing me that you are as human as all of us. I'm thrilled to know that you can also lose your cool.'

I gaped at him! His laughter that followed still rings in my ears.

Generally, I'm known to be genial and ever-smiling—someone who doesn't let off steam easily. Throughout the making of *Annamalai*, things had been smooth and none could have known that I could erupt too. But I am also conscious of the fact that if you unleash your temper too often, it will lose value.

Meanwhile the pulley and rope were brought back. Mani took his position on it and was literally tossed up and down for another two hours before the work regained its lost sheen. Naturally, shooting was delayed.

'See the strain he has undergone to draw it, Sir . . .' I pointed out.

'I completely agree with you, Suresh. But once again, thanks for being like all of us,' he pulled my leg again.

The fan of Rajni who had created quite a flutter on the set had fled the scene, and we resumed shooting well past the allotted time.

20

PENCHANT FOR LEVITY

Rajni loves humour. A good joke or a comic sequence can make him go into uncontrollable bouts of laughter. And once he's in that mood, making him look serious for a shot is an uphill task. When he has to perform a light scene, it isn't easy to make him sport a straight face. He just cannot! If Rajni has to appear serious in a scene where the other actor who is with him has to be funny, the director has had it!

In *Veera,* where he was sharing screen space with Senthil, having him maintain a serious look was quite a challenge. He would go on a chortling spree even as the comedian performed.

Rajni and Senthil are musicians in search of an opportunity to work on an album. They are at the gates of an audio firm—they have to meet the proprietor (played by Livingston), who is sitting in his plush office.

'Sir, you are plagued by problems, financial and emotional. You have left your mother alone in the village, and you are now in the city in search of a job. A huge loan has to be settled and you know that the sharks back home will not spare your mother if you don't return with the money within the stipulated time. So you have to look worried and disheartened as your efforts to find work don't seem to fructify. Senthil will approach the watchman here for information about openings at the office inside. You don't have any dialogue in this scene. You take care of the expressions and Senthil will do the talking . . .' I went on explaining the scene at length. Rajni was all attention and kept nodding his head.

But in front of the camera, every time Senthil began to say his lines, Rajni was in stitches.

'Sir, please understand. You have to look very serious,' I pleaded.

'I know, Suresh. But somehow once Senthil takes off, my laughter becomes unmanageable. Just give me some time. I'll do it,' he smiled.

But time or no time, Rajni couldn't suppress even his chuckles, leave alone look serious, so tickled was he!

After a few futile attempts, Rajni suggested that he could use a towel to cover his mouth, so that his expression wasn't visible. And it worked. Only after the towel was given to him were we able to can the shot. Watch the scene in *Veera* to know the exact situation I'm talking about. You'll notice Rajni's face half-covered!

E laborating on Rajni's timing in comedy is redundant. The Superstar has proved his adeptness at it in innumerable films. Rajni, or rather Muthu, accompanies his first wife to a temple. His second wife decides to visit the same place. Senthil, his friend and confidant, who knows that Rajni is already there with Meena, tries his best to dissuade Roja from visiting the same temple, but his efforts are in vain. Senthil sees no way to warn Rajni (it wasn't the era of mobile phones) and so he decides to accompany Roja.

He dreads the possibility of Roja seeing Rajni and Meena together at the temple. However he does manage to warn Rajni—his sonorous signals of caution are interjected with his chants of the Lord's name as if he is filled with religious fervour, and they help avert the crisis. But his worst fears come true when Roja spots her husband leaving the temple with Meena. Senthil allays her doubt by confusing her so much that, finally, she isn't too sure whether the man in circumambulation in the precincts of the temple along with another woman is actually her husband or somebody else who happens to bear a close resemblance to him.

Yet she has to have her suspicion cleared, so she heads straight for Rajni's office, where he is supposed to be at that very moment, to check it out. Senthil manages to warn Rajni of the impending doom, and realising the gravity of the problem, our hero rushes back to his office to be there before Roja arrives.

The scenes turned out to be unforgettable exercises in hilarity. The exchanges between Rajni and Senthil in the sequence that had the lines punctuated with a loud

'Govinda Govinda' at every turn expressed a wide gamut of emotions—caution, fear, anxiety and finally, relief. Including the chant in the dialogue was an impromptu decision, made just as we were going for the take.

Rajni is a natural. So such improvisations are common when shooting with him. And invariably they work out well. In the scene Rajni is dressed in the traditional dhoti. He tries to flee the place, trips on his dhoti and continues to scamper with the cloth partially flowing down.

We had no retakes for this segment. The cinematographer was on his toes, ready to capture Rajni's antics as he ran around in a frenzied manner. We hadn't planned the minute details. Everything about it was spontaneous and unfolded beautifully, as Rajni enacted the scene with exuberance. I explained the situation and he took off from there in inimitable style!

An admirable characteristic about the Superstar is his yen for humour. He enjoys portraying humour as much as the viewer who watches it. He finds his comic capers so amusing, that you can see him laughing aloud long after the scene is wrapped up!

We didn't have monitors in those days, to go back to a scene soon after it was canned and check it out for ourselves. We had to be satisfied with reliving the moment over and over again in our minds and savouring it. But the point is, the *joie de vivre* that encompassed the entire unit when we shot the comedy scenes of *Veera*, is unforgettable.

We filmed the sequence at the Birla Temple in Hyderabad. Shooting was generally not permitted within the precincts, but we managed it.

Come to think of it, in those days it was much easier to obtain permission for shooting at public places than it is today.

Once inside his room at the office, he has to change from the dhoti that he was in while at the temple, into formals. But when he is at it, Roja enters! Rajni immediately slides deep into his seat—he's still in his underclothing waist down—so that the huge table in front covers him. She tries to go near him but he goes further under the table. His expressions and body language in this scene are incredibly funny. And watching him from behind the camera, I was in splits. My reaction was the same when I went back to the scene later on at the editing room. It was clean humour at its best!

I love comedies. The story of *Annamalai* didn't lend itself to much levity. But *Veera* was so full of light-heartedness that during the making of the film, both Rajni and I had a great time!

When it came to stunt choreography, Raju was always my first choice. Raju Master's fight sequences had a unique style. And unless inevitable, he preferred not to go in for a double for the leading man. Most of the time he would make the hero perform the stunts himself.

We introduced Mahesh Anand as the villain in *Veera*. There is this sequence in the film where he and Rajni jump high towards each other and then fall to the ground with their hands interlocked. Rajni and Mahesh literally flew in the air before they landed in the position they were told to. The two didn't rehearse for the shot. They watched the stuntmen perform and followed their instructions to a T. Mahesh was slightly apprehensive, but Rajni instilled confidence in him saying, 'Mahesh, Raju knows what he's doing. If it were risky, he wouldn't allow us to go ahead. Come on, everything will be fine.'

While editing the film, I decided to repeat the same action in slow motion, because it is very difficult to envisage and execute such shots. I'm talking of the days when no ropes were used to hold the hero and villain securely! Today several gizmos do the trick, but it wasn't so then. The two actors accomplished it in a jiffy, and in the most casual manner possible.

The fights in *Veera*, including the one in the climax that was fought in an auditorium, were done without a body double. It was Rajni himself who performed all the stunts!

As the film began to gain concrete shape, my confidence in the project grew. I realised that the cocktail of action in reasonable measure, the ample dose of comedy and Rajni's charismatic screen presence would take the film to the winning post. Eventually it did turn out to be so, though *Veera* didn't soar high straightway. It took time to gather momentum. Yet it scaled the pinnacle of popularity and success to become another noteworthy hit in Rajni's impressive oeuvre.

Once *Veera* was ready to roll out, I took a break. I was away in Ooty with my family at the time of its release. The film met with a lukewarm response in the first couple of weeks. It was expected because comparisons with *Annamalai* were inevitable; but I was sure *Veera* would be a success. Critics' reviews of the film were mixed. 'Different,' wrote some. 'Not as good as *Annamalai*,' was the verdict of a few others. But in a matter of a few days we saw the tide turning in our favour. It was just a matter of time before Veera began his victory run, after which he was unstoppable.

A week prior to the release of *Veera*, Rajni called for a meeting with the media. Rajni's press meets are always well-attended.

'*Veera*'s release is round the corner. At this juncture, I wish to inform you all that my next film will be for Sathya Movies. And once again I'm going with Suresh Krissna as my director,' he said.

I was overwhelmed. He had already told me about it, yet hearing him say it in front of the Press moved me no end.

'The film will be called *Baasha*,' he announced.

Even today, my heart swells with pride when I think that I was associated with Rajni's evergreen winner, *Baasha*. The unbridled heroism of the protagonist and the unprecedented success of the film are talking points at every proscenium where Rajni's hits are discussed, even eighteen years after it strode into Tamil cinema's hall of fame!

21

THE BEGINNING OF *BAASHA*

After Rajni announced our third project together, the two of us took off to Hyderabad to conceptualise the entire plot. All we had was a single scene discussed on the sets of the Hindi film, *Hum* (1991), in which Rajni had acted with Amitabh Bachchan and Govinda. The scene had impacted the Superstar tremendously.

Mukul Anand, the director of *Hum*, had considered, discussed and finally decided to discard the scene, because he didn't find it suitable. But Rajni felt that it had the potential to be developed into a full-fledged story. The scene in question was as follows:

Govinda wishes to join the police force, but doesn't get admission to the Police Academy. He comes out crestfallen. Bachchan, who is upset to see his brother's unhappiness, goes in to meet the chief there and comes out with a seat for Govinda. What transpires inside the room is a mystery that is unravelled only later.

So when we sat down to write the story of *Baasha* we

began with a somewhat similar scene. Once it was finalised we wove the rest of the story around it. None who has watched *Baasha* can forget the vital sequence of events. Rajni's sister approaches the chairman of the medical college for admission. He ogles at her and suggests she spend the night with him at his guest house in return for a seat in his medical college. The girl leaves the room in shock and dismay and is seen sitting alone in the canteen, inside the college campus, where Rajni eventually finds her.

Puzzled he says: 'The entire family is waiting for you at home, anxious to know the result of your interview, and here you are all by yourself, brooding.'

'No *anna*, I don't wish to study medicine. Let me do a Bachelor's in Science and take up a job,' she replies.

'I know how keen you are about medicine, so stop beating about the bush. Tell me exactly what happened,' sensing that something is amiss Rajni prods her. And sobbing, she narrates the incident.

Seething with anger, he says, 'Come along with me,' and makes her get up from the chair. He holds her hand firmly, and goes to meet the man who had dared to act indecent with his sister. Her plea about the futility of his attempt goes unheard as he storms into the office. The chairman gives a disdainful look and scoffs at the girl and her brother, an ordinary auto-rickshaw driver. Manickam can brook the insult no longer. He asks his sister to wait outside the room and turns to confront him again.

From here on, the conversation isn't audible. The sister

can only see them through the glass door—not hear them. The sudden change in the body language of the thug is intriguing. Through the glass we see him cringe in Rajni's presence. Both his sister who is seated outside and the audience are perplexed!

What can be the clout of an auto-rickshaw driver that has made his opponent show such fear and obsequiousness?

A powerful sequence that remains unforgettable!

It was during a casual conversation on the sets of *Annamalai* that Rajni first talked about the original scene, which had been talked about on the sets of *Hum*.

'How do you like it, Suresh,' he asked.

'Sounds very interesting! And it surely kindles my curiosity. The intrigue is perfect for a suspense drama,' I replied.

Again out of the blue, he asked me one day, 'How do you like the title, *Baasha?*'

'A potent name undoubtedly! And if it is going to be the name of the protagonist, a Muslim connection in the story is obvious,' I said.

'We'll talk about it later,' Rajni smiled smugly and that was it.

In an earlier chapter I'd mentioned that when Rajni called me over to direct *Veera*, I brought up the subject of *Baasha*. But he didn't want to jump into it straight away. He bided his time, and only after *Veera*, did he feel he was ready for the mammoth project.

So, at the time of the announcement of the film, all we had was the scene described above and the title. We were yet to weave a strong and plausible story around it. We decided to allot enough time solely for the purpose and work in right earnest.

Meanwhile, *Veera* had been declared a hit. Rajni took a short break from the grind, and when he returned from his holiday, we were all set to start planning *Baasha*.

Again it was at Taj Banjara—Rajni's favourite hotel in Hyderabad—that we stayed. He loves the enchanting lake view the suites offer. It was at the very same hotel that the screenplay of *Veera* evolved. This time too we decided to ensconce ourselves there, with none to disturb us for the next couple of weeks. We talked for hours on end to shape, chisel and fine-tune the story of *Baasha*. We kept throwing ideas at each other till the wee hours of the morning.

Once Rajni applies himself to a subject, the profusion of thoughts that flow out from his mind has to be witnessed to be believed. He would keep suggesting twists and turns and creating characters that would have a bearing on the story as a whole. And as I work more or less on the same lines, our rapport was perfect. Even as an idea occurred to either of us, we would thrash it out threadbare, retaining the salient features, thus simultaneously sifting the chaff from the grain.

After putting our heads together for days, the smorgasbord of action, emotions and expressions that eventually emerged seemed an infallible scorer!

Thus, with the encounter between the hero and a powerful politician as the pivot we developed a plot that had occurrences before it and after. We built the edifice slowly and steadily. In about ten days we had most of the story, including the flashback in the latter part of the film, ready. But we still had to justify the title, because till this point, the story didn't include a Muslim. We didn't want to even think of an alternative title for the film, though, so we had to work towards making the name 'Baasha' relevant. We found a way soon, and we had nearly eighty per cent of the script ready. The time to bring dialogue writer Balakumaran on board had arrived.

Even at the outset, we had decided that the entire team of technicians of *Annamalai* would work with us again for *Baasha*. *Veera* had included more of producer Panchu Arunachalam's constants, such as Ilaiyaraja. But for *Baasha,* Deva was back. Nagma was the unanimous choice for the heroine's role, as she was reigning supreme in Tamil cinema at that point in time. Films such as director Shankar's *Kaadhalan* had transported her to dizzying heights of fame. We felt she would be a value addition.

Thus the preliminary stage was successfully completed and we geared up for the shoot of the magnum opus called *Baasha.*

22

THE REFRAIN LIVES ON

If the 'Vandhaenda Paalkaaran' refrain in *Annamalai* attained cult status, so did the opening 'Naan Autokaaran Autokaaran' number in *Baasha*. *Veera* didn't lend itself to such a song sequence because the story and characters were in a different league. The genre was romance, and the texture and treatment, soft. But, like *Annamalai,* the story of Baasha warranted a grander, more forceful, song-oriented entry of the hero than *Veera* mainly because *Baasha* epitomised chivalry and valour!

The office of R.M. Veerappan's Sathya Movies, the producer of *Baasha* in Royapettah, Chennai. Composer Deva and I had reached the place ahead of time; we were to be joined by the Superstar, and the verse expert, Vairamuthu.

Rap was a rage then, and hip hop and Boney M a craze. So Deva began to try out something on those lines for the opening song. But it wasn't working out as well as I wanted it to. Noting my expression, Deva said, 'I have an idea. I'll sing a typical gaana (a genre akin to Tamil folk music; Deva revels in it) tune for you. Tell me what you think,' and sang it. I was impressed. And it was this tune that soon got transformed into the 'Autokaaran' song.

The gaana originally composed by Deva went this way:

Kappal paaru kappal paaru
Kappal meley dora paaru
Dora keezhey aaya paaru
Aaya kayila kozhandhai paaru

(See the ship sailing
See the Englishman on it
Also see the poor native woman on board
With a baby in her arms)

I snapped my fingers in satisfaction. 'Our song should be along these lines, Deva. Western beats won't jell with the kind of film we have in mind,' I said.

Just then Rajnikanth and Vairamuthu walked in. We first played the rap song for them, and Rajni's immediate reaction was, 'This won't suit us, Suresh. My fans are sons of the soil. Let's have the kind of music they'll enjoy and identify with.'

'He's right. This doesn't seem like an auto-rickshaw driver's refrain,' Vairamuthu seconded.

'We feel the same way too. That's why we have a back-up ready for you,' I said and looked at Deva. And Deva took off on the gaana trip once again.

Rajni liked it a lot. 'Superb, Deva,' he complimented him. 'But I'm not too sure how it's going to sound in our context.' He turned to Vairamuthu with a smile. 'Now, my dear poet, you know the situation. Give us the lines,' he said, and passed a writing pad, paper and pen to him.

Vairamuthu took up the challenge with enthusiasm. 'I'm game. Give me the tune, and ten minutes time.'

Rajni, Deva and I walked out, leaving him alone. We were chatting over a cup of tea, and presto! at exactly the tenth minute, Vairamathu sent word for us to return to the room! He had the verses on the sheet of paper in front of him and the opening words were, 'Naan Autokaaran Autokaaran!'

'Fabulous job, my dear poet,' laughed Rajni, as his eyes skimmed through the lines. At that very moment we knew we had a hit number on our hands. Vairamuthu's lyric had etched the character of the hero very appropriately, and lionised him aptly!

Deva's brothers, Sabesh and Murali, are wizards at incorporating fresh sounds in a song and ensuring that they make an impact. The reverberating folk beats of 'Naan Autokaaran' exemplify their potential. Together with the chorus of '*Achukku ina achukkudhaan*', the song became a favourite of Rajni fans and auto-rickshaw drivers then, and remains so till date!

The inimitable voice of S.P. Balasubramaniam lent power to the number—few can match the range of his voice or the fire and punch that he lends to lyrics. Pertinent emphases on the words of a fiery and forthright song that help convey the mood perfectly are this inimitable singer's forte. The attribute has contributed to the success of many an SPB song. Among today's crop of singers, Shankar Mahadevan's voice has this kind of power. Equally appealing are the gentle and caressing expressions in his romantic strains.

Even today, ovation reaches a crescendo every time 'Autokaaran' is sung on stage, Deva tells me. 'At all my music shows, I save *Annamalai's* "Paalkaaran" and *Baasha's* "Autokaaran" for the end. The songs help me sign off a show with thunderous applause,' he says.

In fact, all the numbers in *Baasha* were chartbusters. The audio album was a stupendous success, and a special function was organised at Hotel Chola Sheraton to celebrate it. Rajnikanth was presented a platinum disc on the occasion.

Now that we had an appropriate opening song, we had to match it with an equally impressive choreography. That was when Tarun Kumar's name cropped up. Tarun is the son of Hiralal, the famous dance master of yore. Hiralal's footwork for the song 'Yaaradi Nee Mohini' ('Who are you Mohini?') in Sivaji Ganesan's *Uththama Puththiran* (1958) should be still vivid in the minds of many a filmgoer.

In the 1990s, Tarun Kumar's innovative steps for the numbers of Amitabh Bachchan and Govinda were drawing much attention.

Those were the days when Rajnikanth was working in quite a few Hindi films, and hence was flying to Mumbai frequently. Rajni had observed Tarun's work, and had also met him on quite a few occasions. 'There's this person doing splendid work in Hindi films. I think we should try him out, Suresh,' Rajni suggested.

'But we *do* have great choreographers here, including Raghuram who's been working with us for long. If we're bringing someone all the way from Bombay, he must be worth it. He should be able to bring something new to the dances. Let us first see what he can come up with and then decide,' I said.

'Fair enough, Suresh, we'll check him out,' Rajni agreed.

So Tarun Kumar was asked to come down to Chennai. He met us at the office and we played the song for him.

'Give me five days, Sir. I'll complete the choreography and get back to you,' Tarun promised.

Once he was ready, he called us over to the huge empty floor at AVM Studios where he had assembled a contingent of fifty dancers!

That Tarun was familiar with the Tamil cinema scene and Rajnikanth's charisma were significant factors in his favour. In fact, having spent a lot of time in Chennai, he could speak the language too. Hence his choreography was perfect for an actor of Rajni's stature.

Rajni and I were floored by the riveting footwork he came up with. Regular Hindi filmgoers who have watched the subtle and stylish steps of their heroes will find Rajni's movements for the 'Naan Autokaaran' sequence very similar. Tarun had dancers holding yellow scarves and dancing in perfect synchrony. It was an eye-catching display.

Rajni doesn't prefer heavy movements in his song sequences; instead he opts for light twists, turns and twirls, with the accent on style. Tarun seemed to have understood the hero's preferences very well. Rajni was immensely pleased, and so was I. The verve and vitality of the sequence seemed to set in motion the high-octane action that was to follow! The entire six-minute endeavour was replete with gallantry, humour, sentiment and skill, which assured me of its appeal. As expected, audiences were bowled over by the spirited show by Rajni and the rest of the dancers.

A couple of elements added to the popularity of the sequence. Tarun had Rajni walking in just as a pumpkin was thrown high in the air to ward off the evil eye (a common practice at pujas and auspicious occasions). It was made to come into contact with Rajni's head ever so lightly and get smashed into pieces, thus marking the grand entry of the Superstar.

Also, as in the 'Vandhaenda Paalkaaran' song, we had Rajni looking into the lens with a smile, which made viewers feel he was looking directly at them, and putting his hands together as if to greet them. At the editing table, I found the gesture so effective that I extended the screen time of the shot. And it secured the response I sought!

I've already mentioned that Rajni can carry off any costume with élan. None questions the congruity or otherwise of his attire and accessories. When you think of an auto-rickshaw driver, the image that comes to your mind is that of a slightly unkempt person in khaki. But here was the Superstar in a smartly-tailored uniform, sporting a stylish tee and a costly pair of Reebok shoes to boot! It is twenty years since *Baasha*'s release, and none has questioned the costume or the add-ons that didn't quite suit the role!

'Sir, the shoes look too high class,' I began.

'Forget it Suresh, I don't think people will find it odd,' he told me.

And he was right. Rajni knows the pulse of the audience and his charisma, which help him pull off incongruities with ease!

'Naan Autokaaran' was filmed at the open space at Vijaya Vauhini Studios in Chennai, where Hotel Green Park now stands.

Magie, our art director, had erected a massive set for *Baasha* there, which included Rajni's house, the neighbourhood, a theatre, tea stalls and a cycle stand.

Optimum utility of a set of this magnitude is a must, otherwise it affects the viability of a project. Generally, no producer wishes to create a costly backdrop just for a scene or two, because then the cost of production could escalate to mind-boggling levels. The director has to ensure that when a milieu is envisaged, it has enough scope to be used well. And Rajni is a hero who never allows the producer to be over-burdened. I remember dwelling on it while on the filming of the 'Maadathilae Kanni Maadathilae' song in *Veera* when, at the last minute, we changed the way it was going to be shot. Even then Rajni was particular that neither time nor producer's money be wasted.

Going abroad merely for song sequences was a practice Rajni abhorred. Most of his films were filmed in and around Chennai. Nor did he prefer going to places down South. Outdoor shoots, for him, didn't extend beyond Ooty! After *Baasha,* when his popularity graph touched an unprecedented high, he stopped going to Ooty and made Hyderabad his preferred work spot. That Hyderabad too was soon smitten by the Rajni charm is another story!

So it was at the same venue at Vauhini that more than twenty-five vital scenes of *Baasha*, including the 'Naan Autokaaran' song, were shot.

All the dancers who were positioned on either side of Rajni in the first row for the song are ace choreographers today. Go back to the sequence, and you'll notice Kalyan and Ashok Raj, to name a couple. Whenever I meet them, they never fail to talk about the song shoot. It had made such an impact on them because they are all ardent fans of Rajni. They vied with each other to find a place in the sequence! 'We'll cancel our other shootings and be there, Sir,' they told me. There were a hundred of them altogether and the song was canned in four days.

From the moment the song was played over the loudspeaker on the set, none could stop humming it. It was an instant hit among the cast and crew. Even now, at the annual Ayudha Puja, you can hear the song blaring from auto-rickshaw stands!

23

SIGNATURE LINE

The muhurat shot of *Baasha* was filmed at the same venue in AVM Studios which, as I mentioned earlier, has come to be known as Rajni Pillaiyar Temple. Ardent fans of the Superstar had been invited for the event, and they went into raptures on seeing their favourite hero in flesh and blood. The excitement that permeated the air was absolutely mind-boggling.

Most of the scenes that occur in the first hour or so of the film were shot on the huge set at Vauhini Studios. They included comedy sequences, romantic interludes featuring heroine Nagma, and stunts crucial to the film. So we decided we would complete all the scenes that had to be filmed there before we dismantled the set once and for all.

Twenty-three days of non-stop shooting was going on at a feverish pace. The first half of the film had to culminate in a fight between the villains and Manickam, the hero. Shooting was proceeding rapidly, and it was in this particular fight sequence that we planned to introduce the dialogue, '*Naan oru thadava sonna nooru thadava sonna madhiri*' ('Saying it once is equal to my saying it a hundred times'). Rajni doesn't use the power-packed line too many times in the film, but every time he does, force— both physical and mental—emanates from it.

We hadn't incorporated any such effective punches in the dialogue in *Annamalai* or *Veera*, though in the former we had the phrase, '*Malai da*, Annamalai' ('I'm as strong as a mountain, I'm Annamalai'), which we thought would pass off as an inconsequential utterance! But Rajni's voice modulation made such a tremendous impact that it caught on unbelievably! In fact, in the entire film it was used just once, and we didn't expect it to become so popular!

Using distinguishing dialogue for a hero lends potency to the character. Soon several leading men began to have such lines in their films. Punch lines, as they are known in local parlance, became essential to define the heroism of the protagonist. But when we first thought about this line for *Baasha*, we had no idea that it would become a trendsetter and a hallmark of film heroism in the decades to come!

While we were in the process of planning the most important fight, which would showcase Manickam as an unassailable protagonist, Rajni kept telling Balakumaran and me that we have to work it out with care. 'Manickam will reveal a hitherto unknown side of his to the family. Here the dialogue must be succint, poignant and memorable,' he suggested. Simple yet effective, it had to be! Many ideas cropped up but we only drew a blank at every turn. The day of shooting arrived and we were still groping in the dark for the right lines! Eventually, it was Rajni who came up with, '*Naan oru vaatti sonna nooru vaatti sonna maadhiri*', which was modified later with '*thadava*' used instead of '*vaatti*'. Balakumaran and I felt it was bang on!

Only Rajni, Balakumaran and I knew the piece of dialogue. It was the usual ploy we adopted, so we could judge its effect by the response it evoked in the crew at the shooting spot. Even the assistant directors didn't know about the line. I play this trick often on the sets, as I view it as a sample of the audience's reaction. It helps me gauge the likely response at cinema halls later.

Just before going for the take, Rajnikanth, who was rehearsing the words over and over again, called me aside.

'One moment, Suresh,' he said.

'Tell me, Sir.'

'Just listen to this and give me your opinion,' he said, and in his inimitable style continued, '*Naan oru thadava sonna nooru thadava sonna madhiri*. Do you think it sounds better than, *Oru vaatti sonna nooru vaatti sonna madhiri?*' The meaning of the words is the same—'*vaatti*' in Tamil is a synonym for '*thadava*'.

I repeated the two versions to myself a couple of times and then replied, 'You have a point. I think *thadava* has more zing to it. But let's ask the writer,' I replied.

Balakumaran didn't quite agree. 'Why, Sir? *Vaatti* sounds fine to me,' he said.

Rajni repeated both the versions a few more times, loud enough for us to hear and looked at me. I felt he had a point, and told Balakumaran so. Rajni added, 'Balakumaran, I too feel *thadava* sounds more forceful. Let's change it.'

We got ready for the take. The camera whirred and Rajni, looking menacingly at his opponent, said, '*Naan oru thadava sonna nooru thadava sonna madhiri!*'

'Cut it,' I called out with jubilation. I loved the way he said it.

'Super,' screamed everyone on the set. The impact was such that, in the break that followed, everyone was using the words in all possible contexts. I heard an assistant call out for tea and then say, 'I've asked for it once. It means I've asked a hundred times.' 'Get me a chair,' shouted another and followed it up with, 'I've said it once. It means . . .' It had caught on in a jiffy, and to an extent I could measure the influence it was going to have on filmgoers. But not even in my wildest imagination did I envisage it being used so widely by so many people for so long a time! And that, considering it occurs only five or six times in the film! Such, I suppose, is the Rajni effect!

The fight sequence at the midpoint in *Baasha* is a vital part of the narration. The hero, whom everyone venerates as practically a superman, is shown as a timid, trepid guy. He is tied to a lamp post on the road and beaten up by the villain.

Raju, our stunt choreographer, came up with a suggestion. The hero's faint-heartedness prevents him from fighting the thugs who are beating up his brother, a policeman. But being an affectionate sibling, he pleads with the men to spare his brother, and thrash him up instead.

'That way, later, when the hero retaliates forcefully, the impact will increase manifold,' Raju said. We agreed and sketched out the scene accordingly. As I always maintain, filmmaking is teamwork, and worthy ideas can come from any quarter.

I was absorbed in canning the shots when I sensed confusion behind me—a frenzied discussion was going on. Soon producer R.M. Veerappan's son-in-law Ramalingam, who was part of the group that was talking animatedly, called me to his side and said, 'RMV wants to meet you.' It was almost five in the evening—time to wind up anyway, so I headed straight to Veerappan's office. He called me in.

'Please sit down. What scene were you shooting today?'

RMV, as he is referred to, knew only the outline of *Baasha*. We had never spoken in detail about the script.

'Rajni is tied to a lamp post . . .' I began, but he didn't allow me to complete the sentence.

'Are you joking? Do you have any idea about his image and his popularity? The way he is surging ahead reminds me of MGR's star power! The very mention of his name brings applause. And you coolly tell me that you will have him tied and beaten up by thugs! His fans will tear the screens at the cinemas. Please change your screenplay. Villains can't be allowed to bash up the Superstar. I won't permit it in my film,' he said.

I knew that no amount of reasoning would work and left the place without further argument. I drove straight to Rajni's home and briefed him about RMV's opinion of our day's work. Immediately Rajni called him up and said, 'We are coming over to your place right away.'

RMV didn't mince words. He repeated his apprehension. This time Rajni stopped him midway. 'Sir, trust us. This isn't an ordinary script. Only if I get beaten up now, when I pay them back in their own coin later, the impact would double. I have confidence in Suresh. He'll execute it well,' he said. RMV didn't look convinced, and Rajni continued in a placating tone, 'All right, *Baasha* has been planned as a Pongal release (Pongal, the harvest festival in Tamil Nadu, is celebrated in January). I'll show you the double positive of the film on December 15. If you still feel the scene can't go, we'll re-shoot it and I'll bear the cost.'

I was moved by the confidence the Superstar reposed in me.

Very reluctantly RMV conceded. 'All right, I agree, but don't say that I haven't warned you. I'm still not too happy with the idea,' he said.

24

MAKING IT WORK

That entire night RMV's words kept ringing in my ears. An experienced senior like him, who had been a witness to the charisma of an actor-politician of the calibre of MGR, was sceptical about my move. His view had to be given due consideration because he wasn't talking through his hat. He had a valid point.

I stalled shooting for around five days. I needed time to deliberate on my move and discuss it thoroughly with my crew. The evening after our meeting with RMV, I sat for a lengthy debate with cameraperson Prakash and stunt choreographer Raju on the manner in which the scene could be shot.

'We'll tweak the scene so that it appears that Nature is angry at the treatment meted out to a peace-loving person like Manickam. Lightning, rain, thunder, wind—the works,' I said. 'The scene should be dramatic, with backlight and other props. We'll introduce a poignant background number to round off the scene.'

Thus was born the soft, melodic refrain, 'Baasha Paaru ... Baasha Paaru' ('Look at Baasha'), which helped lift the heroism of the protagonist to levels hitherto unseen in Rajnikanth films! Deva did an admirable job of the song, for which Vairamuthu supplied some excellent verses.

Manickam's faithful men from his past who witness their invincible boss being bashed up as he takes it all without a whimper, wish to rush towards the rogues and make them understand the mettle of their leader. Their anger is uncontrollable—one clenches his fist and the other crushes the glass in his hand in sheer despair. They can do nothing more as their leader, Baasha, whom they revere, has ordered them to stay calm.

The brother is bleeding and is completely shaken. He thinks Manickam is a coward to take the blows from the villains lying down. 'Isn't your self-respect at stake? Even a timorous cat tries to claw at its attacker in a bid to protect itself. Aren't you angry with the men who meted out such injustice to you? Haven't you *ever* hit anyone in your life before,' he asks. The irony of the last query in particular was very well received at the cinemas later.

Balakumaran had written a lengthy piece of dialogue as Manickam's reply to the brother. 'Suresh, can we do away with the verbosity here? How will it be if my reply to the volley of questions is only loud, meaningful yet cryptic laughter,' Rajni asked me, and demonstrated the way he could act it out.

'It should work,' I enthusiastically agreed. 'Let's have it exactly as you performed now.'

And as was our wont, none on the set, save the two of us, knew the reaction Rajni had in mind. We canned the scene as trolley shots—the camera moved towards Rajni as he broke into an intriguing, sarcastic guffaw. Here was the man, whose daredevilry had once stunned the Mumbai underworld, being quizzed by his younger brother with naïve questions. The scene was received with a loud cheer, and the spontaneity of the crew was a reassurance that it would further exemplify the fact that Rajni is a show stealer!

Later at the editing table we realised that the length wasn't enough—we needed to prolong Rajni's guffaw. So we made the scene appear a little slower. Instead of the usual twenty-four frames per second, we paced it at thirty-six, because forty-eight frames would have made it too obviously slow. Thus we protracted it a little and got the desired length.

The result was remarkable. And when RMV came out after watching the scene in full, he said, 'You've enhanced the effect to an unbelievable extent. And I have to accept that you've proved me wrong. I didn't expect it to be so dramatic,' he shook my hand.

But the real surprise was when the audience started putting their hands together even when Rajni was being dragged to the lamp post. They anticipated their hero's retaliation, knew he would return the 'honours' blow for blow, and began cheering even when he was being thrashed!

Just before intermission, Manickam warns the thug to beware and lay off, with the words—*Naan oru thadava sonna nooru thadava sonna madhiri*. Words that were to become a gospel for Rajni lovers all over!

25

CLEAR STAND

We had already recorded two duets—'Style Style' and 'Thanga Magan' ('The rich, golden, favourite son')—for *Baasha*. In a commercial film, three is the norm. The composing session for the third number had been completed and only the recording of it remained to be done. Simultaneously, the crucial fight sequence that I've described in the previous chapter was being shot at Vauhini Studios. So while the recording went on in the mornings, the fights were being filmed at nights.

In between the shoot, I noticed Rajni deep in thought. I quietly sat beside him and waited for him to come out of his reverie. He slowly opened his eyes and said, 'I was just pondering over the inclusion of the third duet. Do we need it Suresh? Wouldn't it appear that we are going overboard with the romantic angle?'

It was my turn to ruminate. The first song, 'Naan Autokaaran', marked the hero's entry. The philosophical number, 'Ra Ra Raamiah!' ('Come here, Raamiah') with wordplay on the numeral eight was essential because it culminated in the villain's foiled bid to kill Baasha. 'Style Style' showcased Tarun's masterly footwork, and was hence important. We needed a regular formula song and 'Thanga Magan' filled the bill. So Rajni was probably right. We didn't need another duet . . .

'As the recording is nearing completion, we'll retain the song in the audio alone,' I suggested.

'Fine, let's do it that way,' Rajni said.

I went to Prasad Studio where Deva and his brothers were in the process of completing the recording of the song. It was over at 6 p.m. and Deva played the whole song—'Nee Nadandha Nadai Azhagu' ('Your gait is admirable')—for me. I was entranced by the sheer beauty of the melody, so mesmerizingly sung by S.P. Balasubramaniam and K.S. Chitra.

I rushed back to Vauhini, where Rajni was getting ready for the stunt sequence that was to be shot. I was still in the grip of the enticing piece of music I had listened to at Prasad. 'Sir, I'm just returning from the recording. The song is out of the world,' I said, my voice revealing my excitement.

'What are you implying, Suresh? We decided we won't have it in the film. Let's stick to it.'

'Sir, what's the harm in just listening to it, for my sake?'

'If I agree and come over to the studio, I may be captivated by the tune, just as you are, and we'll return to the point where we began. I'd rather not listen to it,' he said. I sensed a tone of finality in his voice.

'Sir, I still feel you should accompany me to the recording studio, at least for Deva's sake. He has worked hard on the song and if you don't even give it a hearing, it would upset him no end.'

'But it's time for the shot here,' Rajni contended, and I realised that he had begun to relent. Come hell or high water, I had to make him listen to the duet.

'I just spoke to Raju and Prakash. They need another thirty minutes at least to get things ready. We can hop into a car, finish the job and return in a jiffy,' I coaxed him.

'Nothing will stop you from taking me to Prasad, will it,' he smiled and got up.

'My director says your song is great. Can I listen to it now,' Rajni asked Deva. And Deva very happily played it for him. From the expression on Rajni's face, I could make out that he was as impressed with the number as I was. The voices of the veteran singers and the excellent arrangement made it aurally elevating.

'Super,' said Rajni. He congratulated Deva and his brothers, and in the same breath added, 'But we plan to have it only in the audio cassette.'

Deva was shocked. 'Why, Sir?'

'Because we already have two duets and a third could be too much. What, Suresh? Haven't you told him about it?'

'Sir, we'll talk about it.'

'What do you mean, "We'll talk about it?" There's nothing to talk about. The song is good but we can't shoot it,' said Rajni, of course, with a smile on his face, and began walking towards the car. Though Rajni had a strong opinion about the inclusion of the song, I knew that eventually he would leave it to me.

Deva looked visibly crestfallen. 'It's a beautiful melody, Suresh. Why is he saying that we can't have it in the film?'

'We'll see what we can do about it, Deva. He has a point. But maybe if I hit upon an appealing concept, I can make him agree. I'll see how it can be managed,' I tried to pacify Deva.

We returned to Vauhini to shoot the rest of the fight sequence. Neither of us mentioned a word about the song.

As far as an action scene goes, I brief the stunt choreographer about the emotions I need, explain in detail the exact situation in the story when the fight occurs and other relevant aspects that we need to concentrate on, after which I leave it to him. Raju Master and his assistants were still discussing the action when we entered Vauhini.

Rajni, as I've told you, doesn't seek privacy at the shooting spot. Relaxing in a caravan has never been his practice. Once he reports for work, he stays put at the place till the call for 'pack-up'. And as he waits to take his position before the camera, if he isn't closing his eyes for a catnap, he can be seen chatting with the light-boys, helpers and make-up men around him. The Superstar is in the best of moods then—letting his hair down, completely relaxed and cheerful. That evening too, a group had gathered around him and he began talking to them casually. My wife was also there. 'The song is wonderful, Chandra, but we can't have it,' he told her.

She turned to me and asked in a soft tone, 'Why is he saying so?'

'His argument is correct. But still it's a mellifluous piece. I can't allow it to be confined to the audio. We have to shoot it,' I said, and quietly moved away. I had to zero in on a concept for the song. I went to the farthest corner of the set and began to walk up and down, thinking of a way to make the song different and entertaining enough to be included in the film.

Though Rajni would thoroughly enjoy the conversation with others on the set, he would also keep looking for me if I was not around. That evening was no exception. He saw me from afar and commented to my wife, 'I know what he's up to. He's thinking of a way to save the song. Mark my words. In a few minutes he'll walk up to me saying, "I have an idea, Sir",' he had told them and laughed aloud, and the others had joined him.

Oblivious to being the target of fun, when I suddenly had a brainwave, just as he had said, I rushed back to where he was seated. 'What did I say? Look at the sprightliness in his gait. He must have found a way of bringing the song in,' he was telling them when I came up to him and said, 'Sir, I have an idea.' Those around him burst out laughing. I was perplexed but not in a mood to find out the reason. I had to share the idea I had hit upon at once. 'Come on, Suresh! Have your say,' he winked cheerfully. At that point, he was asking me to go ahead only to humour me. As far as he was concerned, the decision about the song was final.

'Sir, Nagma walks into a gym and you are the instructor there. She's confounded and looks around at the others working out. She's flummoxed to see that every one of them is you! Bewildered, she runs out, and the doorkeeper is you.'

Rajni lifted his hand asking me to stop, and took over. 'She walks out in a daze and a marriage procession on the road has me as the nagaswaram player. A rich man alights from a car in front of her and it's me again. And Suresh, I've never played a bus conductor, so let's have that too,' he went on.

Inspired by my suggestion, he unwittingly began to think on similar lines. Soon, each one in the group came up with various characters Rajni could play!

He had got into the rhythm of the sequence and it was my turn to watch his enthusiasm with a smile. He called for Sundaramurthy, our make-up artist. 'Remember the costume I used for the role of a rowdy in *Thappu Thaalangal*? Could we include it here?' he said. Forgetting that he had been very much against filming the song, he began to involve himself completely in the shooting of it!

'I think this will be the best conceived song sequence in the film. Ask Tarun to work on the movements for it,' he said.

Next evening when we assembled at Vauhini to continue canning the rest of the fights, he listed out more characters he could play in the song sequence. He must have been pondering over it the whole night, I thought.

He then looked at me and said, 'I was only against a mere song and dance routine, Suresh. This is one of the most unique song concepts I've worked in. To think that the number I was so against is going to be the best of the five songs!' he laughed.

The visual splendour that was served to viewers was shot at Film City in Chennai. For his part, Tarun included a policeman's uniform and a purohit's attire for Rajni. The zest with which the cast and crew worked for the song was almost palpable! We thoroughly enjoyed shooting the sequence.

'We have a winner on our hands, Suresh,' he complimented me without any reservations. He turned to my wife and said, 'Your husband is great! What a superb idea he has come up with!'

26

DESTINED TO BE IN

Every time I listen to 'Style, Style', I recall actor Sathyaraj's words. 'It's easy to pen a lyric for Rajni, because everything about the Superstar spells style. Describe his gait, mannerisms, hairstyle and smile and you've got the verses ready. His fans find his expressions and movements unique, and the numbers filmed on him, extraordinary. Duet, montage song or solo, fans don't see a Rajni number as a pace breaker, because the accent is still on his style and the heroism he embodies. He's their inimitable Superstar. The ploy doesn't work as effectively for other heroes, including me,' he told me.

The rapport that a director and composer share can go a long way in making the songs in a film appealing. Deva and I always have a wonderful time working together. Music continues to bond us. I'm an incorrigible music buff, and I listen to all kinds of music.

Just the other day, I was clearing my cupboard full of

audio cassettes. When the task was completed, I realised that I had accommodated them in four large suitcases and there were still many more! Obsolete though they have become, I couldn't part with them easily. Wherever I am, be it the dining table, car or my room, music has to be on, always.

I love music in all its genres and languages. I listen to Punjabi, Gujarati, Marathi, Bengali folk and melodies. Songs from old Hindi films are a passion and semi-classical is a favourite genre. When I travel I collect private albums unique to the country, and my collection includes rare strains from places such as Sri Lanka and Thailand.

As music is an obsession, I listen incessantly and jot down the names of tunes that appeal to me. When Deva and I discuss its various forms, I play my collection for him. In turn they inspire him to create original tunes. We are an egoless twosome. He likes to listen to my list of favourites and I like to listen to his reinventions and experiments with music. I can attempt this kind of sharing of tastes only with Deva. He understands my passion for the art. Not every composer would appreciate it if I play my choices for them.

'Thanga Magan' is a brilliant composition from Deva. We decided to have Yesudas sing it. Soft numbers are Yesudas's forte. His rendition of the melodious 'Oru Vennpura' number in *Annamalai* became popular with every stratum of viewers. This time we wanted to offer him a soothing, semi-classical piece. It was to be the last song in the film, and we planned to lend it a very different visual feel.

27

GREEK GRANDEUR

As mentioned earlier, Rajni's lean and lanky frame helps him carry off any costume. That was why we decided we would make him sport the attire of a Greek warrior, for the 'Thanga Magan' song. When I told Rajnikanth about it, he hesitated. 'Let me be frank, Suresh. My legs are thin. Honestly, such an outfit won't suit me,' he said.

When equally interested parties put their heads together for a project, various ideas could emerge. It's the same when a director and a hero sit down to work out the tasks ahead, and the strategies. Each uses the other as a bouncing board and when it happens in a healthy ambience, the consensus they reach pays off. So when I realised that Rajni wasn't too happy with the costume I'd suggested, I could understand his point. Our aim was the same—to make a film that would be a treat for viewers. So my next thought was to find a solution that satisfied both of us, because working in a friction-free atmosphere is always primary. Finally it was decided that he would wear trousers. He agreed and the matter was solved. As I said, Rajni can get away with anything! None raised an eyebrow about our Greek warrior in drain-pipe trousers!

The set that art director Magie had erected for the sequence was aesthetically Grecian. (I cannot forget the visual brilliance he had created for *Veera*. We had gone with Chalam for *Annamalai*.) Inspired by Magie's artistry, dance master Tarun accentuated the appeal further by having all the dancers literally painted in a golden hue! They looked like bright statues moving around elegantly—it was enchanting.

Little aware of the hurdle that awaited me at the editing table, I sat absorbed in the beauty of the song sequence that was being filmed.

I t was when we sat down to check the length of the entire film that we realised that the 'Thanga Magan' song sequence was playing sleeping policeman, halting the velocity at which *Baasha* was otherwise moving. Did we need such a speed breaker at all? The question was met with a vociferous, 'Let's cut it out.' But I couldn't let go a sequence that had been so painstakingly conceived and created. 'I'll think of a way to use it, and I'll see that it doesn't impede the pace,' I said.

We had inserted the number at a crucial point in the story—Rajni storms into the crowded marriage hall where Nagma is being forced into wedlock with her father's crony. He walks up to the dais, clutches her hand and stomps out with her and none, including her father, dares to stop him. After which the couple breaks into a song.

Very soon I hit upon an idea. 'We'll start playing the song even as the two begin to walk out of the hall,' I said.

'Yes, then it will not stand out as a separate song sequence but as a continuation of the serious scene,' chorused my editors Ganesh and Kumar. Our excitement was back. We were going to retain the melody after all!

So finally we had shots of the song as intercuts and the audience saw them as an extension of the emotional and intense scene at the marriage hall. Of course, we also edited the song and made it very tight. Thus we had our cake and ate it too!

The popular number 'Style Style' was incorporated mainly to showcase the Superstar as the king of style. The choreography, costume and set were all created with the charisma of the actor and his impact on the audience in mind. Plaudits for the footwork should go entirely to Tarun, who used the Superstar's magic to the maximum.

The make-up, including the beard, blazer and the pince-nez, on Rajni in the flashback that dealt with his days as Baasha was a huge success from the very first time he wore it. The pince-nez was make-up artist Sundaramurthy's idea, and it lent incredible uniqueness to Rajni's appearance. The look urged me to go in for a song sequence with him in the costume, but Rajni vetoed it straight away.

'Baasha is a serious man Suresh! How can you even think of making him prance around?'

I wasn't willing to give up, though. 'Maybe we can have a suitable context. It would go a long way in making the character memorable. Every time you think of Baasha, you would think of the song too,' I argued.

'But how? He can't walk around singing and making merry. He is a man with a mission—his only aim is to pulverise the power of his enemy, the man who has killed his dear friend! He's a very serious character. Don't bring him down from that position,' Rajni said.

'I won't. But there has to be a way,' I replied.

'Like?'

'Like a situation where he uses a song to convey a strong message to the villain—that he knows the enemy's game plan and is armed well enough to counter it . . .' Even as I spoke, the concept began to take form, just as it happened when I started talking about the 'Nee Nadandha Nadai Azhagu' sequence.

The villain's henchman has been planted in Baasha's camp to stalk and kill him at an opportune moment. Raghuvaran played the don Antony, and Devan, his crony.

I thought I should insert a song there. 'Let the sequence be shown as part of Devan's plot. Pretending to be obsequious and loyal to Baasha, he organises a birthday bash for him. The idea is to kill him at the party. A song sequence and the action it leads to should be intriguing,' I told Rajni. He liked the idea.

The lyric for the song had to be written. Usually, Deva would compose a tune and give it to Vairamuthu, who would then write the words for it. But this time we felt we would go about it the other way. Vairamuthu would get the verses ready and Deva would set them to tune.

Now for the subject of the number. Rajni couldn't possibly sing a song wishing himself on his birthday! Neither can it be shown as a day of revelry for him! It should have a lyric that's philosophical, meaningful to the situation and witty, all at once. Otherwise it would fall flat and like Rajni feared earlier, appear ridiculous! We were breaking our heads for an appropriate theme to build the song on when Rajni came up with an idea from a Kannada poem. It was as apt as the concept he had given us earlier for the 'Vandhaenda Paalkaaran' song in *Annamalai*.

'This philosophical poem splits up the average number of years in a man's life into compartments of eight, and dwells on the significance of each,' said Rajni.

The cue was enough for Vairamuthu. 'Putting it in lyric form is a challenge. I'll try,' he said and sat down to work on it.

Remember the famous 'Raamiah Vasthavaiyya' number

in *Shree 420*, the Raj Kapoor–Nargis hit of 1955? It had made a lasting impression in my mind. I thought of it and suggested 'Raamiah' as the opening line for this philosophical strain and everyone found it suitable. Thus was born the evergreen song, 'Ra Ra Raamiah! Ettukkulae Ulagam Irukku Paaraiyya' ('Raamiah, come and learn that life in this world is divided into segments of eight').

The opening lines of the song, which are in Hindi, are my small contribution to the lyric, and they go like this:

Ek hi chaand hai raat ke liye
Ek hi suraj hai dhin ke liye
Ek hi baasha hai is jag keliye

(The night has only one moon
[And] The day, one sun
[Similarly] The world has only one Baasha)

Before we began shooting the song, we discussed the execution threadbare. Using eight candles and bringing in fire to add to the aura were Tarun Kumar's ideas. His choreography for the number still remains an outstanding part of the song. The movements he introduced were very much like the footwork of heroes in Hindi films, particularly Amitabh Bachchan. In fact, the dance as a whole, with its Marathi folk beats, is so reminiscent of a Big B number.

28

MEMORABLE SHOT

Generally, filming isn't done in the order of sequences that they appear on screen. It is taken up according to the convenience of the hero's dates or depending on the availability of the locations decided upon. But surprisingly, shooting for *Baasha* was taken up almost in the order of the narration. The first schedule, which happened in Chennai, on the huge street set at Vauhini studios, including the main action sequence till the midway point in the film, continued till the entire first half had been completed.

The rest of the film, which was to run as a flashback in the second part of the film, beginning with the introduction of Baasha, and the other scenes with his rival and enemy Antony (Raghuvaran), were to be shot in Hyderabad and Mumbai. Baasha should first be seen by the audience in the backdrop of the Golconda tombs in Hyderabad that were under the ground level, we thought. An imposing location befitting the introductory scene of the formidable Baasha!

From there we decided to move to Mumbai and shoot the major scenes involving Baasha and Antony, such as the scene where the two meet at the Gateway of India, as the effort would give an authentic look and establish that Baasha hailed from Mumbai.

Our first stop was Hyderabad. Rajni and I kept discussing the scene over and over again, because it was the most crucial part of the film. In the first half we had vested the character of Baasha with potency and authority through three vital scenes: firstly when the DIG of Police respectfully stands up to receive Manickam, the innocuous auto-rickshaw driver, realising him to be Baasha; secondly when the college chairman is shown wiping the perspiration on his forehead and cringing in the dominating presence of Manickam, as he presumably talks about his past avatar; and thirdly when he explodes in anger against the brutes who attack his family. We had made the audience wait long enough and now we had to showcase Baasha's supremacy first hand.

The makeover from an ordinary, diffident man to that of a dreaded don had to be striking. So how is Baasha going to look?

We had decided to shoot the scene in the dark hours before dawn at the Golconda tombs at 2 a.m. The entire team of technicians with Prakash and Magie had left early to complete the lighting and get the props in place.

Make-up artist Sundaramurthy, costumer Sai and I were at Taj Banjara Hyderabad, watching Rajni prepare himself to appear before the camera. After make-up, it was time for him to get into his costume.

Normally, if Rajni is in the make-up room, we can be assured of a rip-roaring session. Joy, camaraderie, friendly banter . . . Rajni is in the best of moods then. Actors, producers and directors from the neighbouring set would visit him or he would invite them over to join him for breakfast or lunch. I wish I had shot those moments that reveal the real Rajni. Fun-loving all right, but also sincere and down-to-earth, when he would talk about his vicissitudes in life, working as a bus conductor and the initial stages of his career when worthy roles and sufficient payment were hard to come by. The anecdotes which cross my mind now are innumerable that I can go on and on. I cherish those moments, especially his no-holds-barred chortle, that would end up in tears of laughter rolling down his face.

But on the first day that he got himself ready to play Baasha, the don, he looked very solemn and serious. It was a different Rajni that I saw. Absolutely quiet, he was too preoccupied to even notice the presence of others, leave alone chat with them. Seeing him so, those around him also fell silent. They realised that the hero was getting into the skin of his new character—Baasha.

Slowly he got up and started checking out the costumes Sai had lined up for him. He took them out one by one, placed it on himself and stood before the huge mirror to see which outfit suited him best. I was watching him and liked what I saw. A committed actor who was giving the character he was to play his all. I could see Baasha grow in stature right in front of my eyes!

Finally, Rajni chose a black suit that had a brown design on the coat. He took his time wearing it, all the while looking at himself in the mirror. The intensity on his face seemed to be increasing, as if he was gearing up to face the camera in full form, as Baasha. And when he stood in style in the suit, it was as though he had completely transformed into the sober yet dynamic Baasha! What a sea change from the appearance of the poor auto-rickshaw driver he had been in the first schedule of shoot!

He then wore his shoes, and even as Sundaramurthy was styling his hair further, Rajni kept looking at the mirror and I understood he still found his appearance wanting. He turned towards me with a blank expression because his thoughts were on finding a way to better the look of Baasha. Suddenly he asked Sai for a scarf and threw it round his neck. It definitely enhanced the look. He asked those around him to move away, switched off all the lights, except that above the mirror and took a few steps up and down. He was happy with the result, but still not entirely so. That was when Sundaramurthy came up with the suggestion that Rajni should sport a pince-nez with shades. Rajni plumped for the idea; it was brought and when in his typical style he tried it out and removed it, he looked satisfied. He then looked at me. 'Fantastic,' was all I said.

I left for the shooting spot ahead of Rajni. Everyone,

including Prakash, was eagerly waiting to catch the first look of Baasha. 'He is on his way. Wait for some more time,' I smiled.

And when Rajni entered, I could make out that he had wowed them! Prakash look at me and said, 'Super!'

Now to the scene ... We canned some shots of Baasha walking inside, near the tombs underground, as a build-up to the vital scene. Prakash had lit up the place excellently with yellow lamps that danced in light and shade. The actors, who were to play his henchmen, were suited and booted and stood behind Rajni, looking stern and menacing.

After cranking the shots that had him walking up and down, it was time to shoot the crucial scene, his first appearance as Baasha. Rajni's taciturnity continued and none of us disturbed him. He was deep in thought and we let him be. It was as though the entire unit was waiting with bated breath for the arrival of a VIP!

Rajni called me over to discuss the scene, and surprisingly, during the conversation, his voice turned hoarse, just like Baasha was supposed to sound in the film! The look was sharp and piercing, just as we had envisaged for the character of Baasha. It wasn't Rajni, the actor who was talking to me—it was Baasha himself! As a director, the experience was thrilling! What more could I have asked for from my hero who got so involved in his role that he even began to sound like him!

After the other minor shots had been canned, Rajni, or rather, Baasha, had to attack the enemy's underling who had been caught and tied to a chair for his boss's sinister design. He had planted a bomb in a busy suburb of Mumbai where a religious celebration—the annual Ganesh festival—was on. Hundreds of devotees had converged on the place and they could get killed if the bomb wasn't located fast. Getting wind of the enemy's plan, Baasha's men had swung into action and had managed to catch hold of one of the suspects. Only he could tell them where the bomb had been placed.

The scene opens with Janakaraj, Baasha's trusted lieutenant in the film, interrogating the enemy's underling. Baasha watches silently, but soon realises that the man is lying and the time to save the crowd is ticking away . . .

At this point, Rajni had to turn around in his chair and walk towards him menacingly. He stopped and looked at me saying, 'It would be better if I could sit on a revolving chair now. It would make a better impact than my getting up from it and walking towards him.' Magie needed just five minutes to find one, and being an art director with acumen, he also managed to bring a long plywood plank to be placed under the chair, as the uneven ground near the tombs would not allow the wheels to move smooth and fast. This way the wheels were on even keel and Rajni could swirl around in his chair, and move it so that it skidded and stopped right near the actor who was being questioned. Rajni was happy with the change made.

We went for the take at once, because I was not for a rehearsal. I knew Rajni had got into the skin of the character and rehearsals could hamper the mood. I instructed Prakash to begin with a long shot and slowly close in on Rajni. Prakash nodded and I went up to Rajni and whispered in his ears, 'This is the shot I'm banking on to make Baasha explode in all his fire and fury. Your eyes and body language can achieve it.' Rajni was a picture of concentration. He heard me out, and went for the shot.

And what a shot it was! As Rajni stylishly slid forward in his revolving chair, looked intently at his opponent and said, '*Naan oru thadava sonna nooru thadava sonna maadhiri*', I watched him spellbound. The power of Rajni's eyes that became increasingly piercing, his telling expression and impressive body language were stunning. I sat entranced and forgot to call out, 'Cut'. It has happened to me a couple of times earlier too, when directing Rajni. Prakash slowly turned his eyes towards me, puzzled because I sat mesmerised and mute. Only then did I realise the impact Rajni's performance had had on me, and hastily wrapped it up. The applause on the set that followed seemed an apt culmination. A significant shot, which deserves to go down in the history of the making of *Baasha*, because it was at that moment Baasha was actually born ... The look and demeanour of Rajni as Baasha had been carefully chalked out, but the execution of it began with this particular shot.

Later that evening after pack-up, when Chandra and I were driving back to the hotel, we couldn't stop talking about the shot. As a token of our appreciation, we decided to send Rajni a bouquet, and in the card on it, I wrote, 'Today Baasha is born. What a performance! Electrifying! We are waiting to see the myriad facets of Baasha . . .'

And true to my wishes, scene after scene, Rajnikanth went on to perform in an amazing fashion that far exceeded my expectations . . .

I still remember producer and distributor Ananda Suresh's comment after watching the film. Referencing the Tamil remake of the Hindi film *Don*, starring Amitabh Bachchan, he said, 'Suresh, we have seen Rajni the villain of the *Billa* days, whom everyone found endearing. *Baasha* brings back those memories . . .'

29

EXUDING POWER

Every member of a filmmaking crew contributes to a film's overall success. So when the main technician is singled out for recognition in the form of awards, the work of the others could go unsung. That's the reason why I've recorded the inputs of everyone in the projects that Rajni and I worked together! I hope this book has redressed such anomalies and given credit wherever it is due . . .

At this point I need to touch upon Raghuvaran's portrayal in *Baasha*. An excellent character actor whom Fate has snatched away from us! He vested the role of the main villain with class and dignity. He is one anti hero who didn't have to be loud or physically imposing to look menacing. Without much ado he could give the impression that he was powerful enough to take on any hero. Raghuvaran's screen presence was terrific, and his eyes and voice were assets.

Devan, Raghuvaran's henchman who turns against him and is the cause for his incarceration, is casually browsing through a newspaper in the comfort of his palatial home when his eyes fall on a news item stating that Raghuvaran has escaped from prison. He is shocked out of his wits because he knows that the man would head straight for his house and go for his jugular. He slowly lowers the paper in his hand—and sitting right in front of him is Raghuvaran himself, looking at him with an evil glint in his eyes.

When we shot the scene I was mesmerised by Raghuvaran's expression. To this day, the scene remains vivid in my mind's eye!

As a performer Raghuvaran emanated power of unimaginable magnitude. Whenever I was involved in a Telugu or a Tamil film, I looked for a suitable role to bring the ace actor on board. Be it the soft elder brother in *Aaha* (1997), the schemer who spews venom in *Baasha* or the insidious chicaner in *Oruvan* (1999), Raghuvaran was my first choice. A very courteous person, a good friend and an excellent actor, I truly miss him.

In the entire first hour or so of *Baasha*, the protagonist isn't shown as a powerful hero. A Superstar whose action sequences are eagerly looked forward to and lapped up remains practically chicken-hearted in the early part of the film! The idea was to tantalise the audience and then serve heroic action to saturation.

Manickam, the hero, is like a dormant volcano waiting to erupt. And when the moment arrives, he hits back, and how! Having kept the audience waiting for quite a while, it was only appropriate to provide a sumptuous meal in the form of powerful action.

When you consciously push yourself to think harder and do better, you could draw a blank. That was the position I was in.

The first fight sequence in *Baasha* was to appear rather late in the film, and it *had* to make a tremendous impact. Emotionally, the sequence had been built up to a crescendo, with the sister being pushed around literally, and the mother and brother being beaten up. How could I bolster it up further, I wondered. The simmering fury of the hero had to burst out into fiery, uncontrollable action. So I decided that the point of retaliation would begin when Rajni's sister is rudely thrown into his arms, with her lips bruised and blood oozing from her mouth, after which he isn't going to take the brutality lying down any more. A picture of pusillanimity dramatically changes into a personification of puissance! Everyone in the neighbourhood, including his own family, is shocked at the transformation of the soft and silent auto-rickshaw driver into an angry, invincible hero!

The fight sequence was choreographed after much thought. I wanted it to affect the audience in a way that would make it memorable, and I was glad it did. An attacker rushes towards Rajni. A single punch and he is sent hurtling against the lamp post at a distance; he falls to the ground with a thud. The camera pans to the shocked faces of all those gathered around and then zooms in on Rajni as he pushes up his sleeves and menacingly moves towards his enemies. To make it more effective, we added a series of dissolves. The musical and visual build-up enhanced the dramatic impact, and the beats punctuated with intermittent, vociferous sounds of 'Hey, Hey!' worked magic!

The sibling, who is physically hurt and mentally shocked by the happenings around him, tries to go to Manickam's help. But his deep-throated command of 'Move out' makes him freeze with fear and confusion, at this new, hitherto unseen facet of his brother. Manickam then pulls out an iron hand pump near him with unbelievable potency to strike the enemy. His five faithfuls who have been with him from his Baasha days in Mumbai, are at the spot, waiting to close in on the enemies. But seeing Manickam's reaction they stop midway.

I wanted it that way because, otherwise, their intervention would have reduced our attempt to showcase the protagonist's unbridled heroism. Raju Master went on adding more blows and punches. It was as though Manickam was unstoppable. Yet by cinema standards it wasn't a high-octane action sequence, because we didn't have much blood and gore in it.

Once we finished filming the scene, the crew congratulated me for making Manickam explode so fiercely. No doubt, the scene lionised Rajni to a great extent. Yet I wasn't completely happy. I still kept thinking that something more could be done. Obviously I couldn't have huge cars rolling over one another or helicopters descending from high above to attack as in a James Bond film.

I realise now that these weren't necessary. If the scene is remembered even a decade and a half later, it is because of the emotional slant we lent it. Probably, another reason was the way in which Baasha's pent-up fury was unleashed in one go. The audience wanted him to strike back, and when he did the euphoria was complete.

30

THE WAY IT WENT

The entire film, as I mentioned, was pegged to the encounter between the chairman of the medical college and Manickam. As it was the pivot of the narration, I had visualised a huge set with glass doors, opulent décor and a magnificent backdrop. 'We'll take a lot of time and execute it with care,' I had told Rajni during our earlier discussion. 'The scene warrants elaborate treatment.'

On this particular day, we had planned to can a few scenes at Film City. All of us, including Rajni, were ready, but the lashing rains didn't allow us to proceed with the shoot. We waited, as the downpour continued without let-up.

Rajni called me to his side and said, 'Suresh, instead of wasting time, shall we begin shooting some of the indoor scenes?'

I wasn't prepared. Also, the actors required for the scenes which could possibly be filmed indoors weren't present obviously because we hadn't planned to shoot their scenes that day.

We had canned the scene with Yuvarani (who played Manickam's sister) and Rajnikanth at the canteen inside Film City. We were all set to move outdoor next, when the rains began and continued relentlessly.

'Let's not waste time, Suresh. Let's do something,' Rajni urged.

I thought for a moment and said, 'We've planned to shoot the two scenes in the chairman's room at a special set we intend to erect . . .'

Rajni stopped me midway.

'Why not finish it here and now?'

'Yeah, but . . .'

'Come on, Suresh! Let's do it.'

I began to feel it could be done. 'If we can get the room that's being used by the Film City chief director Madhavan, and ask Sethu Vinayakam (the actor who was to play the medical college chairman) to come over here at once . . .'

'Good. Then go ahead and tell them to get the room ready,' Rajni said cheerfully.

It was noon. 'We'll break for lunch and then begin the lighting,' I told the crew. Meanwhile, Sethu Vinayakam was sent for.

By the time things were set up and we could go for the first take, it was two in the afternoon, and we had to wind up at six! We had just four hours to shoot three vital scenes — Yuvarani's first meeting with Sethu Vinayakam, which ends with her walking away with tears in her eyes, her second entry into the room with Rajni, which includes the potent and popular piece of dialogue beginning with, 'My name is Manickam. But I have another name too . . .' and the smooth flow of the scene into an intriguing one-to-one meeting between Rajni and Sethu Vinayakam (when you don't hear the words exchanged), which is witnessed by the sister from behind the glass door of his office. The suspense would be revealed much later.

An uphill task by any standard of filmmaking, but I went ahead!

When the camera was set for a wide shot, we captured all the three scenes from the angle and when we went in for close-ups, it was for all three again. None of the shots had continuity, but I went on, because I knew what I wanted . . . Thus the shooting of the most important scenes in *Baasha,* which eventually began only at 2.30 in the afternoon, was wrapped up by six!

It was at the editing table that the scenes were completely re-constructed. But what mattered was the terrific impact they made. Without exception audiences all over were floored by the power of the Superstar's style, enunciation and expression in the scenes!

The accomplishment exemplified the fact that if the maker has clearly envisaged the scenes beforehand and keeps running them in his mind over and over again, he can overcome contingencies on the set without tension.

Of course, there's always room for improvisation, so ideas that come up after the shoot can probably find a place during editing.

Baasha was completed. We had promised producer R.M. Veerappan a screening, and it was scheduled for that evening. Meanwhile a preview was organised for Rajni at eleven in the morning, and I watched the film with him. Through the first half of the film, Rajni's face glowed with happiness. 'Very nice, Suresh, it's really very nice,' he smiled. We then settled down for the rest of the film. He sat through it silently and when we got up at the end of it, I could sense that he wasn't very enthusiastic.

The editors of the film, writer Balakumaran, Rajni and I were the only people in the theatre. The others thought it was fine, but Rajni looked terribly disconcerted. I waited for him to come out with his opinion. I had anticipated his reaction, so I didn't say a word. And he didn't either. He just got into his car and sped away.

The look of Manik Baasha that was to appear later on in the flashback was very different. The blazer, the pince-nez, the wig, the beard—every item added to the dynamism and style of the character. Rajni looked every inch the Superstar! He liked the costume that had been accessorised to perfection. And in his enthusiasm felt that none of the scenes of Manik Baasha should be cut out or pruned. I understood his mind set, when he told me, 'Don't touch any of these flashback scenes, Suresh. I want every shot to be retained. Manik Baasha is the selling point of the film.'

His child-like eagerness prevented me from arguing with him. Of course, Rajni had essayed the role of Manik Baasha with such sincerity and suaveness, that every shot was like a tasty delicacy. But in his enthusiasm he got carried away, and I was left with little choice. I worked with the editors on the first half alone and left the second as it was.

R.M. Veerappan was to watch the film at six in the evening, and Rajni had left without a word! I kept running the film over and over again in my mind and knew exactly the scenes that had to be trimmed and those that had to be taken out. I waited for Rajni to call me up about our next step. 'Let him take some time, mull over it and get back to me. I will not disturb him now,' I thought.

It was around one when Rajni left the theatre at AVM. I waited till 2.30 p.m. but there was no word from him! Time was running out and I couldn't wait any longer. So I decided to call him up myself.

'Sir, you left without saying anything . . .' I began.

'The first half is excellent, but there's something drastically wrong with the second. RMV is going to watch it in a few hours from now. I think we've made a mistake, Suresh.' He sounded low and dejected.

I felt it was my turn to speak up. 'I'll be very honest with you. This is our third project together. You know me well. A film may have many scenes I personally like a lot, and similarly you may have those that are your favourites, which you consider indispensable. But finally it is the entirety of a product that is most important. Even now it isn't too late. If you allow me to edit the second half of the film, I can start right away.' I was confident I could do it, because I had already completed the editing in my mind.

An admirable trait in Rajni is conceding that he could be wrong. Not every hero of his stature would admit to a mistake. Besides other qualities, his simplicity and honesty are also reasons for his being placed on a pedestal high above others.

There was complete silence for a moment. And then he asked, 'Can you do it by this evening?'

'I can, Sir! I'm already clear about the segments that have to be chopped. Not to worry,' I said. I knew I had a herculean task on hand. As always it was going to be a mad race against time!

'All right then. Go ahead and see what you can do,' Rajni replied in a resigned tone. He had already concluded that we had a flop on our hands . . .

31

HUMBLING EXPERIENCE

Once Rajni gave me the go-ahead to edit the latter part of film, I rushed to Gemini Colour Lab. These days, with Avid in vogue, editing is done at a fast pace. But with Steenbeck, which was in use then, it was a time-consuming procedure.

The speed at which I worked that day still surprises me. How did I manage it, I wonder! Removing a few scenes, pruning some, always with an eye on the logical continuity of the sequences, and viewing the edited parts again to ensure that important points in the screenplay were intact, I went on at a maddening pace. I was working on three editing machines simultaneously. The momentum of the first half of the film had to be maintained, and the narration had to flow smoothly on to the second without upsetting the equilibrium. The work was voluminous and time was at a premium, but it had to be done.

'Why are you cutting out so much, Sir,' chorused editors Ganesh and Kumar. But I was firm.

'It has to be so. At no point can we allow the tempo to plateau out,' I told them. Even amidst such frenzied activity, new ideas to better the impact of certain scenes occurred to me, and I kept incorporating them!

The clock struck six. RMV landed at AVM Studios with his wife and his son-in-law to watch the film, and I was still at the lab working! I sent the first half, instructing my assistants to go ahead and begin the screening. Rajni was also there. But once he learnt I was still at the editing room at Gemini, he rushed to my side.

'What's happening, Suresh? I couldn't find you there,' I could sense the angst in his voice. 'The show has begun. Have you completed editing the rest of the reels,' he went on.

As I've said, nothing ruffles me easily. Equanimity has helped me scale odds with ease and conviction. I knew I could handle this situation too.

'I'll be there with the rest of the film. I will sit with RMV and watch it. Don't worry yourself too much. We can do it, Sir.'

'Are you sure things will work out fine? You've managed to set things right, haven't you? You are confident that the second half too looks good, aren't you?' His anxiety made him shoot a volley of questions.

'Relax, Sir, and be reassured that it's going to be great. What we've done has made it fabulous.'

I had never seen him look so tense. I truly felt that, after so much of sincere toil, we were bound to reap a rich harvest. But I knew that my hypothesis would hardly convince him at that juncture. And if he stayed on with me, his anxiety would only get aggravated.

'Sir, you please go back to the theatre. I'll follow you in half an hour,' I requested. He relented because he realised he couldn't take the stress any longer.

After Rajni left, I made some minor corrections that were pending and followed him to AVM. He was waiting for me outside when I entered. I was in time—RMV was still watching the first half of the film . . .

Once the film reached the midpoint, recess was announced and RMV came out all smiles. 'Great job, my dear young man! The film is thoroughly engrossing, just as you promised,' he patted me on my shoulder. 'I know the second half will be even better.'

Rajni and I exchanged meaningful glances.

The moment RMV moved away, Rajni looked at me.

'What will happen, Suresh?' The edginess in his voice moved me no end.

'I'll be seated beside you. Let's watch the rest of *Baasha* together.'

He seemed slightly pacified but his anxiety was still very evident. The lights dimmed and the screen went up again. As the film progressed the air became lighter. He held my hand tight and the grip told me that his confidence in *Baasha* was back. He leaned back and began to relax. His apprehension had been laid to rest.

Till the end of the show, my attention was only on the Superstar. I was watching his reactions and body language from the corner of my eye. But I could also sense that *Baasha* had floored RMV.

After it was over, an ecstatic RMV came out and walked towards me. 'Excellent! The film has transcended my expectations. It's bound to create records at the box office,' he went on. After calling over every technician to his side and complimenting them personally, he left. I heaved a huge sigh of relief.

The next moment, Rajni turned around and caught me by the collar as if in a scuffle! 'What did you do in the editing room, Suresh? How did you accomplish this magic?' he said, and gave me a hug. He was delirious with joy!

I replied with a smile, 'Sir, the character of Baasha is like a very delicious sweet. A little too much of it could make you feel queasy and uncomfortable. A little less of it will make you crave for more. I've served just the right amount, for you to taste and savour. You will want more of Baasha and leave with a sense of yearning. That's the impact I want, and we've achieved it.'

A film can be made or marred at the editing table. *Baasha* is a classic example. The film's editors and I were able to separate the cream from the other layers to make our dish healthy and wholesome. We had to curb our urge to add all that we found absorbing. The result was the viewer was left pining for more and it made him go to the cinemas over and over again to watch his favourite Baasha in action. And each time he returned because he didn't feel satiated.

It's sheer joy to watch Rajni when he is terribly excited. He was in such a mood after the show. Pacing up and down the hall, he queried, 'Do you know that I was completely distraught this morning? I felt so disappointed that I kept asking myself where we could have gone wrong. *Baasha* is finished. It's all over, I decided. I've made a mistake and I have to face the consequences, I told myself. Then I come here depressed, and you throw this wonderful surprise at me!' Rajni kept repeating the words.

Eventually he calmed down. 'A small request, Suresh. Can we add this particular shot alone? I think I've done a good job of it.' To me he appeared like a small child asking for another piece of chocolate. Here was the Superstar, whose look is people's command, sounding so innocent, and requesting me for a small inclusion! I was stunned by the simplicity of the man! A humbling experience indeed!

'Sir, we knew the crux of the problem and redressed it. A few additions and deletions here and there can be done as we fine-tune the film for the final time,' I smiled.

He laughed aloud . . .

32

REMINISCENCES

During the recent Assembly elections, people from various political parties who came canvassing for votes spoke to me only about *Baasha*.

'It's been more than seventeen years since I made *Baasha*. The Superstar has done many films after it, and I've directed other films too . . .' I began.

'But nothing to beat *Baasha*, Sir. We've watched it a hundred times and we still haven't had enough of it,' they chorused. The sentiment, as I stated earlier, isn't new. To all Rajni fans out there, I'm synonymous with *Baasha*. To this day, no interview of mine, for both the visual and print media, opens without queries pertaining to the making of *Baasha*.

Baasha is an inseparable part of my life. And Rajnikanth is an unforgettable human being, whom I've been lucky to work with in a hat-trick.

I'm not in regular touch with the Superstar mainly because I know that he prefers to have his space. I don't thrust myself on him.

He is a very private person. He loves solitude. His frequent trips to the Himalayas, his penchant for philosophy and his deep study of religious texts are too well known and need no elaboration. But his way of life when he isn't shooting or travelling is an intrigue that fascinates me!

I've had the good fortune of visiting the rooms of this admirable recluse, both at Poes Garden in the heart of Chennai and at Kelambakkam in the outskirts. Almost bare, his rooms have nothing to indicate that they belong to the reigning king of cinema! His room at Poes Garden has a bed, which is more a bench, hard and sturdy as a piece of rock. The shelves are stacked with books on spirituality, and a mirror is placed at one end. That's about it!

His room in his cottage at Kelambakkam is completely secluded. I happened to see it when I was there for the shooting of *Baba*. The only addition is a microwave oven. A high wall surrounds his room, which abuts a swimming pool and a spacious garden outside. It is like a fortress. Food is kept in the room before six in the evening, after which nobody enters. The servants and others are in the outer wing, which has another wall around it.

Rajni spends his time swimming, reading, listening to music and meditating. He heats up his dinner and serves it himself. That is his world, a milieu to his liking! Probably the serene ambience re-charges him enough to carry out his responsibilities as a family man and matinee idol.

When I fully know that he prefers being left alone and doesn't particularly wish to have people trampling on his toes, it is only fair I respect his privacy and his preferences. However, I make it a point to meet him every Diwali. And on his birthday each year, I send a message. Our bonding is based on cordiality and understanding and continues so to this day. I don't impose myself on him. I'm invited to the functions at his home and I have great regard for his wife. My daughters have been students of her school, Ashram.

Recently, Rajni asked me to come over for discussions with his daughter Soundarya, regarding the making of *Sultan*, along with writer S. Ramakrishnan. For nearly two months we sat together and worked on the script. Later, I made my version of the narration and gave it to her.

Embarking on a project without much planning, racing against time and deciding matters off-the-cuff seem to have worked for me. That these are unacceptable ways to make a film is a fact—but in my case such attempts seem to have paid off. This is not a justification, just an observation.

In cinema, each is running on a different track; the track could be smooth or rough, well-laid or bumpy, but reaching the winning post is the aim.

Every few years, questions, conjectures and speculations about a sequel to *Baasha* keep coming up. Even as I write these lines, such talk is doing the rounds. When Rajni has given several other hits, it is still *Baasha* that heads the list in his success scroll.

Soon after his *Padaiyappa* was released, Rajni and I did discuss the possibility of making *Baasha 2*. Even later we discussed the feasibility of the idea. But every time so far, we've only come to the conclusion that *Baasha* should be left alone; that the blaze of glory and triumph should remain a one-time affair. We felt the magic of *Baasha* is inimitable—not even a sequel can equal it. Also, Rajnikanth doesn't believe that sequels work in Indian cinema.

Rajni called me up one morning. It was soon after the release of *Baba*.

'Can we meet?' His voice sounded cryptic, and as always I went over immediately.

'*Baasha 2*—what do you feel about it, Suresh? I know we've discussed it before, but I've been thinking about it and now I feel it could work.'

I nodded in assent and we started working out a few leads to take the storyline forward. Rajni brought in his brother-in-law and actor Ravi Raghavendar, and the three of us had a brainstorming session.

Gen Next steps in. The story, a revenge drama, takes place abroad. Villain Raghuvaran's son returns . . . as we began exchanging ideas, I slowly got the feeling that the trail was worth the pursuit. But Ravi wasn't too enthusiastic about it. 'There's bound to be a comparison.

Will we able to handle it? Rajni fans have awarded a cult status to *Baasha*. Can a sequel scale higher,' were some of the doubts raised.

Once I heard them out, I became sceptical too. 'Even if there's an iota of diffidence, it's better to scrap it, Sir,' I told Rajni.

So we did.

Still, maybe a sequel will be made in the future. Maybe I'll be a part of it, and maybe Rajni's star power would carry *Baasha 2* to the zenith. Maybe . . .